CHURCH HURT, Hands That Prey...

Thomas L. Hampton II

Copyright © 2023 by Thomas L. Hampton II

All rights reserved.

No part of this publication may be used or reproduced in any manner whatsoever without prior written permission of the publisher, except as permitted by U.S. copyright law. For permission requests, contact Adam Convoluted, lwabundance@currently.com

Adam Convoluted is a division of Sahu Media Publishing Group.

ISBN: 979-8-218-30963-3

The story, all names, characters, and incidents portrayed in this production are fictitious. No identification with actual persons (living or deceased), places, buildings, and products is intended nor should be inferred.

Book Cover by James T. Egan, Bookfly Design LLC

Table of Contents

Preface i vii

Introduction viii xxviii

You've Been Hypnotized 1 12

The Alchemist 13 40

You Touched Me, But Hurt My Child 41 60

Unlearn Fear 61 67

Removing The Fig Leaves 68 86

A True Love Story 87 105

Why Do You Look Like That 106 116

The End 117 124

PREFACE

Have you ever wondered why you have been taught that darkness represents evil, sin or even wickedness? Maybe you've been taught that darkness is where dangerous animals lurk. Is this perception of darkness true or is it a learned and accepted behavior and response to the unknown? Suggestion has a key role in what we believe about darkness. Our concept of darkness today comes from our primitive ancestral beliefs forged in a world when there were more dangerous animals seeking prey than were humans and cultivated neighborhoods, villages, and townships. Today, we continue to be plagued and influenced by superstitious belief systems of people who lived in a vastly different world than we now live. When most people lie down to rest at night, they turn off the lights in their homes to create an atmosphere of darkness, quietness, and peace. There is a term in psychotherapy known as Cognitive Reframing, which is a technique used to shift your mindset so you're able to look at life from a different vantage point. A technique which really causes you to step back, examine your course of life, beliefs, influences and even the created reality we live in, and reframe those things with a different set of eyes. We should use this technique concerning our beliefs of darkness. Darkness should be a moment in our busy lives where we steal away from our noisy, mundane norms and prepare for tranquility, peace, and rest but we've been influenced to believe since childhood that monsters lurk in the night. Early man had to face wild animals which hunted prey at night and this adapted fear has been passed down many generations and is affecting modern man today who lives in a much different world. What is it about the darkness that causes fear? Try this experiment, go outside in your backyard during the daylight after a long day of work and sit quietly in your favorite lounge chair and listen to the peaceful sounds of wildlife and enjoy their melodic sounds of happiness and freedom, how peaceful this is. Try this same experiment in the same backyard during the pitch blackness of night, it is very possible that you will have a vastly different experience. You are in the same backyard with the same wildlife but there is a different experience, why? Because darkness covers the sky, and your physical sense of sight is compromised by the darkness, leaving you to imagine the causes of the sounds you hear. It is not that the environment has changed, but there remains a lingering suggestion about darkness in your mind, it is our minds that most frighten us. In this moment, you are left to face the thoughts and creations of your own mind. In moments of darkness, peace and quietness, man must face the recesses of his own mind and that's what frightens us. Uncontrollable thoughts during the moment of darkness in your backyard created your environment. Let us therefore turn within ourselves, reframe our thoughts, and appreciate the peace and tranquility of darkness, control our thoughts, and use our minds to create environments and worlds we would like to live in. **Do not call conspiracy [or hard, or holy] all that these people will call conspiracy [or hard, or holy]; neither be in fear of what they fear, nor [make others afraid and] in dread.** *Isaiah 8:12*

Don't hate them for what they fear, they have been blinded by religion, they have become puppets of a system of theology, and they can't live for hopes of death, that they might die and after death be with Christ. Have you heard of the term heaven bound but no earthly good? What does that mean? We have been taught how to live-in Heaven but are dead to peace and tranquility on earth because we are not convinced that, God is In Us. We've been taught how and what to fear but not how to be rulers of our own minds. What a difference it would make had the learned behavior of fear been replaced with I am Great Beyond Measure; would not Isaiah's prophecy have more meaning in the land of the living rather than pointing to a time after death? Or maybe it will be after the Mental Death of the old mindset and resurrection of the New Mind that, *"The wolf will live with the lamb, and the leopard will lie down with the goat. The calf, the young lion, and the fatling will be together, and a Child will lead them."*

They will no longer live in fear...

'Unlearn Fear and live!'

Are you a victim of the system of things? Why have you allowed yourself to become a victim? Don't blame God, blame the pastor, don't even blame the pastor, blame the system. No, don't blame the system either, come let us together blame our parents and the children go free. People can only benefit from the resources that are available to them at a particular moment. In that moment, decisions are made, and those decisions are usually for the moment, not for life. You've probably heard it said, I've done the best that I can do with the knowledge I had at that time! Why are you blaming me, I was the victim! I did the best I could do, what else do you want from me? If I knew better, I would have done better! I went to church to find the answers, but it seemed like all they wanted was what they could take from me, so I've left the church. Stop jumping from church to church trying to find the right pastor and church home and Find Yourself, then you can have church. It is only when a man searches within is God found, not in a man-made building. No wonder you are a victim, you expect man to build what God already has Some pastors have been influenced by the doctrine that the Holy Ghost had to come from outside of them, it is my persuasion that the internal Spirit is awakened by the knocking... Knock, and the door will be opened. Not the door of the church building... Do you remember standing outside of the church doors until the deacons finished singing those terrible sounding antiquated hymns? Why do you think they would repeatedly crucify us with that horrid sound? The spirit should have told them that the times had changed, a new song was needed to minister to the people. They too were stuck and not free, they were waiting on the spirit to come from the outside of themselves. The Spirit gives life, and the Spirit lives in them, while they were locked in the upper room, waiting for the Spirit to come, who is leading the church? When the physical building has been torn down, you should have learned how to have Church inside. If you were a victim as a child, quit looking outside of yourself for hurting people to heal you. Where do we get our understanding, ideas, and concepts of ourselves? We get them from interacting with people and things in our environments. The change in you, changes the environment outside of you... Many of us believe that to become a better self, we must change physical things, but this is not always the case. To become a better you, change your Inner Space and watch the transformation of your outer space.

"Enlarge My Territory oh God!"

Your territories will be expanded as the world in you expands, not one stone will be left standing of that old, limited environment built by man when the self becomes known.

When Christ is born in you, your Mansion will appear!

INTRODUCTION

    This book has finally found you and this by no accident. The reason you're reading this book is because you have been led to this book. Just as this book has found you, you will find yourself in this book. You are probably thinking that the hands that prey is implying physical hands of the clergy or some other religious figure. This book is about far more than Church Hurt caused by a man in a long robe, having an affair with that lady who loves to sit all the way down in the front row of the church wearing that short yellow frock, knowing she is blessed with so many assets that it makes men and women alike forget why they went to church and what the day's message was.

    Not to mention the stress she puts on that thin dress as it struggles to hide what's been passed down to her from generation to generation; Sister Lily, when you walk, you strut! Girl, I can't believe she comes here every Sunday looking like a Jezebel. She knows everybody is looking, it doesn't make any sense for a Christian to dress like that. Girl, if I had a figure like that, I would show it off too. When you are built like that you can't hide it, no matter what you wear, if you don't like it, stop looking. If you don't have to jump to put your jeans on... No, if you have to jump to put your jeans on, you need to go up a size. Besides, if these men wouldn't look, she wouldn't dress like that. They say they're here to worship God, it seems like they are here worshipping Lilith. No, this book is about much more. *(Lily, short for Lilith, the woman of the night; Adam's mythological wife)*

You have not come upon this book by accident. At this point in your life, you are living on purpose because you have decided that what has happened in the past is the past and everything has worked out for your good. In fact, you are who you are because of your past and the person you are now is the person you are supposed to be. Someone once told me that there was a time when growing up all he wanted was central heating and air because during his childhood, he would get dressed on frigid winter mornings, standing in front of a wood stove and kerosene heater. He would often have the lingering scent of kerosene on his clothes what seemed like all day long. He told me of times when his family didn't even have running hot water in the house, taking a shower was nonexistent. His family would have to heat water on the stove, pour it in the bathtub and bathe that way. If I were writing to you of a time from the 50's or 60's, you may be able to relate, but this was a reality as late as the late 1980's. Coming out of this, and finally living in a mobile home with central heating and air, he and his family are now living the good life.

Like the scent of lingering kerosene, we have the lingering memories of our past which haunt us or liberate us. The lingering effects of negative experiences can cause us to appreciate the small things of life, or we could find ourselves living with a false sense of accomplishment. I'm not in this or that situation anymore therefore, I've made it and I'm living my best life. Just because you've been living in a box, doesn't mean the world is a box. Just as plants and animals become conditioned by the environment in which they live, our lives sometimes appear as if conditioned by the deranged mind of a mad scientist.

Like bacteria in a petri dish, our growth is controlled by the dish, the dish creating our limited mentalities and small-town experiences. I say small town, not because of a limited population of the physical town but because of limited and specific experiences to which a person has been subject.

Just like the bacteria in the dish, the mind is limited by to what it is exposed. To what we have been exposed remains unknown until we come face to face with someone who lives in a larger dish than our own, it is then that we see ourselves for who we really are, it is then that we see the conditions upon which our false and limited realities have been built. It is not until we put off the psychological bars of religious indoctrination that we are set free from the mental prison of where God lives and what group alone is privy to God.

This is not a book of religion; this is not a book about God, but we must start here to get to the root of the laying on of Hands That Prey. It is very likely that the hands that touched you in your childhood still have a hold of your adult mind. In fact, to some extent, those who have been mentally, physically, emotionally, or sexually assaulted, in some degree, have the suppressed mindset of an injured child. Did you know that the brain develops throughout adulthood in a way that reflects childhood experiences? (In America, 5 children a day suffer some form of abuse or neglect, and faith-based abuse is not accounted for in these numbers because **most people don't recognize spiritual abuse until adult hood.**)

In fact, in response to the injurious act, from that day forward until healing occurs, the child will have had to become someone else. The injured person who lives is the altered ego, a second self or at least, a different version of oneself lives. The person who lived before the injury had to become numb in a sense to maintain wholeness. Yes, there was a form of death as a coping mechanism to conceal the childhood pain, you became someone else as you attempted to bury the hands that touched you. Many people are not familiar with the ability of the mind to protect and to project. I call this projection power of the mind, Psychological Adaptation, when you become who you need to become to survive and the person you really are, is suppressed until you decide it is safe to reveal the real you again.

It's Time... Time for Your YOU to live again.

Have you ever been touched in your adult life and heard your injured inner child yell out in terror and pain? Are you yet being touched by the hands of the past? Those hands are still touching you even after 20 or more years. The person has long since gone away but you can't tolerate your husband or wife touching you there. Don't do it like that! What did I do? When you do it like that, who does it feel good to? Well, that's how I was raised. Raised by who? It's a long story, a story that I've never shared with anyone. Something I saw and heard as a child... As a matter of fact, it was more than what I saw, it was what actually happened to me. Who am I married to? Baby, it seems like you are reacting to a stranger.

Often, I wonder if when you are with me, you are thinking about someone else. Why do you say that? I'm not cheating! I'm not saying you are cheating but it seems like you are being touched by someone else, I see fingerprints all over you. Why are you so rough and violent? Did you have a rough childhood? It's like we never talk about anything, it's always an argument!

Damn! Were you abused as a child? Well, we've all been told that we are sinners right... Isn't that what the Bible says about us, we are sinners... well what do you expect from me?

Let me ask you something since you want to criticize me, why do you seem so detached, and without feeling? It's like you don't have any emotion... Do you love me?

Please baby be patient with me and help me heal. There is something I never told you... When I was just a child... (sobbing begins).

No, wait a minute, I need to call my girl about this! Girl, I need to talk to you. What, what's going on? *Sobbing begins...* Girl I think James is a peeping tom. A peeping tom? What in the world? Yes, I woke up in the middle of the night and he wasn't in bed. I looked out the window and saw him crouched down next to the neighbor's window. Girl, I don't know what to do! What's wrong with him, did something happen in his childhood? He needs help! Girl, we all need help, it seems like all of us are going through something. Well, I do remember he said he had something to tell me about his childhood, but I didn't think it was this bad. He told me that when he was in elementary school, one night he got up to use the restroom and had to walk through his mother's room, but the door was closed. Since the doorknob was missing and a "hole remained" where the knob was, he peeped through the hole and saw his mother's best friend and Clarence doing something that scarred his young eyes for life.

What were they doing? Well, to this day, he's obsessed with a certain figure, a body type... Often, he stays up all night watching adult T.V. while I lie in the bed alone. It's not his fault that he was scarred... right? He was just a child, and besides, where was his mother? Oh, she was sleeping on the living room sofa, she let them use her room while her own children were sleeping in the next room. Now, don't forget that we're talking about a pastor's daughter who got put out of the house at 17 for getting pregnant. What? Wasn't he known for preaching the message of Calvary? You tell me where generational curses come from...

Right here is where our journey begins, and those hands of bondage are removed. The past is gone and those who hurt you are somewhere enjoying life, why are they still touching you? Oh, I know, those suppressed feelings of past hurt are still being carried around and show up in every relationship, don't they? You even tried going to church to get a fix but found out that those robes are nothing more than fig leaves, covering shame, they too are wearing garments of their own past.

What if the source of your pain is the church? Then, what do you do? You are not alone, in fact, many people never heard these abusive and degrading words until they attended church; "Nothing good can come from you, you are all worthless sinners, good for nothing and deserving of death!"

Nope, it wasn't your enemy who told you that. No, it wasn't that schoolteacher who hated you since the third grade, and neither was it the town drunk who you would make fun of as you passed his house on your way home from church. It was your Pastor and your parents who quoted those words to you, and not only did they speak those debilitating words over your life, but they attempted to explain how it was God as the co-signer who sealed it with His stamp of approval.

I still remember the scripture they used to validate their misunderstanding; it was Psalm 14:3- *"All have turned away; all-alike, have become corrupt. There is no one who does good, not even one."*

Unfortunately, they did not take the time to see to whom the author of the Psalms was speaking. All they would have had to have done was look at the 1st verse, David was talking about fools who did not believe in

God. Then in verse 5, David says God is with those who are righteous. If none are good, who then are the righteous?

It's time to break free from what has always been, if what has always been, has been injurious rather than beneficial, debilitating rather than invigorating, limiting rather than liberating, ***a whole lot of shouting in church but no shifting.***

Religion is a ritual of beliefs and practices which bind like-minded people together in worship of an agreed upon deity. The key word being bind, we cause our own suffering by what we choose to bind ourselves to. What else would cause a parent in the name of God to put their school-age daughter out of the house for making poor decisions? In fact, research has shown that there is a major difference in the part of the brain responsible for reasoning, planning, judgment, and impulse control in adults compared to adolescents known as the Prefrontal Cortex.

This part of the brain is still developing in teens and doesn't complete its growth until approximately 23 years of age for girls and 25 for boys. It is very difficult at the least for this age group in their early to mid-20's, according to researchers to make good decisions concerning what is safe and what is risky. Those with undeveloped prefrontal cortexes tend to experiment with risky behaviors and don't fully recognize the consequences of their choices. However, countless teens are put out onto the streets to fend for themselves for making poor decisions by church loving parents who believe that God decrees for sin to be dealt with harshly even if it means damaging generations of their own children and grandchildren.

    I often wonder what would've happen if God would've dealt with these parents the same when they too made poor decisions in their 20's. Think for a moment how we send our teens off to college on their own before they are able to think critically. Even children who are sent off to positive environments, such as private college campuses, paid for by loving parents are apt to make poor decisions, what happens to those who have no support from their parents and are placed in adverse situations with undeveloped or no critical thinking skills for survival? Now, let's add to this equation a teen with a baby, since this is the subject at hand. What happens when options are few?

I know of several ladies who were placed in this situation and some of them turned to men they thought would help them, not just one man but man after man and failed relationship after failed relationship to find the love of the mother and father they never knew. It is pure misery when options have run out and a person's only option is to be in a forced relationship.

One of the most powerful truths spoken by man was written by Henry B. Parkes in his book, *Gods and Men, The Origins of Western Culture*. Therein he said,

> "All cultural systems eventually fail because of this one fact. Human energies cannot permanently be contained within the framework of any particular organizational system. [Building] Any such system contains within itself the seeds of its own destruction, for by promoting individual freedom and rational thought it must always bring about the gradual erosion of the institutions and beliefs upon which its stability depends."

In my own words, when man knows the Christ within, he outgrows the physical systems from which he came [Nazareth]. The physical cannot contain the Spiritual Evolution of the Traveling Man, I call that

Traveling Man Melchizedek, the Christ from Nowhere... See the book, "ADAM Man Convoluted, but GOD".

Church Hurt, Hands That Prey, takes you into the lives of those who have looked to man and the church for answers to life's ills but have in turn been further damaged by ignorance, discrimination, greed, indoctrination, false practices, hate and lust within the doors of the church building. In fact, a minister and pastor once told me that he learned how to curse and drink from other seasoned preachers who did these things and were still able to get up Sunday morning and preach.

The author of this book has had his own experience with church officials. As a candidate for pastorship of a Baptist church in Atlanta Ga, during an interview, one of the deacons of the church asked him why he wanted to become a pastor. At the time, he was a single man looking to pastor "God's flock". Considering his single status, the chairman of the deacon board said these explicit words, in the church building as he sat before the 5-member selection board, just feet away from the communion table. "You are a single man; do you know that these church women will f_ _k you to death?" After that experience, he never attempted to pastor another established denominational church again but instead, started his own Interfaith Ministry, **Living With Abundance Ministries...**

That chairman spoke from his heart that day based on what his reality had become after years of his own pain and discouragement from witnessed ruined marriages, adulterous and unnatural relationships where the righteous met every Sunday to have church... His name was Mr. Johnson, chairman of the deacon board... **Church Hurt!**

There was a lady full of love with a heart of gold but molested and abandoned as a child. One day her children returned home from church, a place she felt they should attend but a place she no longer valued for herself. As her daughter approached the front door, she heard a different church at home, it was several minutes before the door was opened, so she waited. What were you doing in there, the little girl asked her mom? Her mom replied as she caught her breath, I was singing a song with Mr. Johnson, and he wouldn't let me move until his song was over. What do you think happened to the psyche of that child as those sounds replayed again and again in her impressionable mind? She could not get rid of the sounds, so she learned to make her own music, she became that which she hated...

'You Touched Me, But Hurt My Child' Mr. Johnson...

We have all heard of the Jim Jones tragedy of Gayana where thousands lost their lives in the mass suicide of Jonestown where the believers drank from the cup of a mad man. How about those of Waco Texas where David Koresh in the 80's convinced intelligent men and women that he was the messiah and that they should sacrifice their little girls to his demonic spirit of pedophilia and even today's stories of people giving to the church while their own bills go delinquent. Have you ever put thought into how this brain washing gradually causes the people to put all their rational thinking aside and trust in man? Well, it begins with "God said".

Once we are made to believe that a particular statement, request, ceremony, or ritual comes from God, rational reasoning ceases and the leader gains support as if the literal mouthpiece of God. Let's briefly look at a religious ceremony which many participate but only a few understand its superstitious and pagan origins.

Communion... Drinking the blood of an animal, god or

man with hopes of possessing its spirit, strength or attributes, believing that drinking of the blood gives life. Viewed in this light, it sounds disgusting, doesn't it? Not only does it sound disgusting, but demonic, considering what the Bible says about consuming blood. Leviticus 17 says, *"Therefore, I say to the Israelites: None of you and no foreigner who lives among you may eat blood. Any Israelite **or foreigner** living among them, who hunts down a wild animal or bird that may be eaten must drain its blood and cover it with dirt. Since the life of every creature is its blood, I have told the Israelites: You must not eat the blood of any creature, because the life of every creature is its blood; whoever eats it must be cut off. They must no longer offer their sacrifices to the GOAT-DEMONS that they have prostituted themselves with.*

I remember preparing for one of these ceremonies in church back in 2011, but as I was reading the opening scripture, a word came to me asking, "Is this what I require?" Although I was the minister reading the scripture preparing the minds of the people to ingest blood, I could not participate. *Since that day, I no longer participate in any such ceremonies.* There is a name for the drinking of blood which dates further back than any biblical history. As with most ancient practices, no one's sure when, where, or why people started using human blood as a religious ceremony, but the earliest documented practices of consuming human blood come from Greek physician-philosophers and ancient Rome by whom Jesus was believed to have been crucified (one image destroyed and the false image perpetuated).

Listen carefully, the image we now have of Jesus came from Rome. Please understand this question. Is this Image that we now have True? The man they once hated enough to murder in the worst way, ask yourself how easy it would be for his message to have been perverted. Why would a man's murderer write his biography to honor him? One final thought on this subject. Ancient man was very fearful and superstitious, and the mere fact that they would witness a man being torn to pieces by a wild animal and watch life leave that man's body as his blood pours from him, it was natural that the irrational primitive mind would conclude that the blood gives life. Since blood then is the life-force, consuming the blood of a fallen warrior, strong beast or god, would endow one with the life.

As late as the 15th century, it is said that *"Louis XI of France and Pope Innocent VIII drank the blood of young boys for their health and strength."* Richard Sugg author. **They are fascinated by little boys...**

The understanding I want you to gain is of crucifixion. Crucifixion was capital punishment, when convicted of a crime deserving capital punishment, that person's name was not to be mentioned in a positive light, he was an eternal enemy of the state, even his family were put to shame, he was forgotten about, and disgraced, not Glorified...

The custom of consuming blood has always had a magical and mysterious meaning. It was used as a part of witchcraft, as a symbolic connection of the powers of life and death.

Your great grandmother's resources were limited, she used what was available to her... **What's Wrong with Your Pan?** *Do you think or do you think you think? Have you thought about where these beliefs and superstitions come from?*

Have you ever been told that to desire wealth and prosperity is evil? This author was never taught how to manage money or the importance of credit and investing because that's what sinners did, especially since we were all dying one day, and heaven is where we should look to prosper and not on earth. Such was the belief of those who nurtured me, God would take care of us basically like he did the Israelites, feeding them manna in the desert. Although he gave us a brain, we weren't supposed to use it to think. Just walk in faith and your dream life will come after you die. Even though God said to Adam, by the sweat of your brow shall you eat your food. Sweat of brow meaning the power of thought which causes the hands to build, not necessarily my hands but those who do not use their minds, the workers will be my hands, mine will never get dirty, you've felt their hands before...

They are owners of million-dollar companies and their hands are as soft as warm butter.

Those who refuse to use their minds will be my slaves and I will rule over them because they have been indoctrinated to believe in heaven and hell and the importance of getting a good job, being a good citizen, going to church on Sundays, coming back home to eat a good dinner, not saving anything for tomorrow, for only God knows what tomorrow will bring. Yeah, but who is this god? The reason this god has taught this foolishness is because it is he who benefits from the indoctrination of the people. He knows what tomorrow will bring for those deceived by faulty doctrines. While he and his family prepare for tomorrow by manipulating the minds of the unprepared, for tomorrow they will work for us. They don't sit back and wait to see what tomorrow brings, they plan for tomorrow today by ordering and commanding tomorrow to bring forth more fruit than they had yesterday.

They are the ones on the doorstep of the courthouse looking at public records every Tuesday morning while the religious people are paying tithes on Sunday morning and losing their houses on Wednesday morning because the church must vote on it Thursday morning to help them save their house.

I am not mad with the church, the church is not an entity that can corrupt itself, the church can only be corrupted by corrupt man. I am the pastor of Living With Abundance Ministries.... so, I am not against spirituality or faith, I'm not opposed to other religious beliefs; Islam, Buddhism, Judaism, Taoism, Mormonism, etc., or any other faith or denomination because I do not practice religion. I am of the same persuasion as Jesus, in that I believe he was a man like me who understood what it feels like to come from a blended family or other than typical family dynamic.

When Jesus was talking to the pharisees about their father Abraham, the Jews said to him, "we know who our father is." They were expressing their belief in the infidelity of Mary, since Joseph wasn't his father. (*John 8:19-59*) This is why Jesus could relate to drunks, prostitutes, tax collectors and the fatherless, not just the isolated fishermen who we know as disciples, Jesus understood people from all walks of life.

Get to know him, the "Man Jesus" and then you may be just like him, as God, he does you no good...

YOU'VE BEEN HYPNOTIZED...

Franz Anton Mesmer, (1734-1815) was a physician, lawyer, and theologian who gave us modern day hypnosis. Known then as a magic spell or even as Mesmerism, hence the name Anton **Mesmer** for mesmerize. He developed the theory of animal magnetism, a belief in the existence of a natural energy force that is shared amongst animal and plant life to include humans. The magnetism which emanates or is shared between beings and can influence actions and reactions consistent with the force.

We've been hypnotized, the wrong religious practice has mesmerized us, and we all are on the same choir, under the influence of his gospel with a little "g." The greatest of the ancient kingdoms were familiar with this occult magic used to create a trancelike mind state, Egypt, China, Mesopotamia, and Rome. Read this very carefully, it describes something very closely related to the science of mind control and suggestion. There is a story of Mr. Mesmer healing one of his patients suffering from convulsions by using only a magnet, hypnosis, and a bucket.

During these convulsions, the patient would feel as though blood were rushing to her head causing her to experience debilitating headaches and toothaches. Anton created within her the feeling and belief that he could remove the blood from her head. He persuaded her that the magnet could pull fluid from her head, to drain into a collection container, and by means of a magnet, a bucket and evidence of collected fluid, the patient never experienced toothache or headache pain again. *The magnificent power of suggestion on the Mind...* Did the healing come from the magnet pulling fluid from her head or did her healing come from what she believed about the man and his symbols?

The Mind is powerful beyond belief, if only we would master the tools of it; the sum-total of Conviction and Speech is the Flowing of life...

Franz Mesmer used a device; the magnet, the power of the human mind and a trancelike state to extract a desired effect from his patients. We are subjects of this same animal magnetism; we have been psychologically and spiritually molested and are all in some way in need of unlearning the past.

Demons...

What plagues us are not some malevolent spiritual beings, what plagues us is our acceptance of learned behaviors which are injurious to our own happiness and growth. Our demons are but learned behaviors, we learn behaviors by interacting with people and situations of life. Let's look at where it all began, just because we've theologized a story of symbolism, metaphors, and similes to convey deeper meanings of life, doesn't take away its author's purpose.

In Genesis of the Bible, we read of Adam and Eve interacting with a serpent who beguiled them, causing them to lose everything they had. Well, another way to look at that story is to see in it a principle of life. When you associate yourself with serpents, you acquire serpent behaviors and ideologies. The life they led after that relationship with the serpent revealed how we are all interconnected and are influenced by others and that when we accept as truth doctrines, beliefs, and practices, we assimilate a new identity.

My teacher would always say, monkey see, monkey do. The serpent was used in this story to describe the power relationships, words and suggestions have over those who subject themselves to what they see, hear, touch and taste. We should all be careful of what goes into us. Don't let any and every one pour into you, we become children of the fallen when we eat their food. Think about the spiritual sense of the word children, offspring, and product. There is another story in the Bible that has been mistranslated and has us believing in giants as well as demons. It talks about the "sons of God," which are interpreted to mean angels by many; Jesus was also a son of God.

Take a moment and think without church indoctrination and see sons of God as righteous or spiritual children. Well, the story goes on to explain that the sons of God saw that the daughters of men were attractive and these "angels" as sons of God have been interpreted to mean, came down to earth or made themselves visible with physical bodies and had sex with female human beings. I wonder why the female angels never felt the need to lay with mortal men, are there no attractive men on earth? However, the story continues;

and from these unnatural relationships, giants or Nephilim were born. This is a learned and accepted religious belief, the church has taught us that, giants once lived on earth.

A Different Perspective...

Jesus replied, "Are you not in error because you do not know the Scriptures or the power of God? When the dead rise, they will neither marry nor be given in marriage; *they will be like the angels in heaven.* This story is found in the Bible in the book of Matthew. Speaking of angels, Jesus said, when men become like angels, there will be no need to marry. We marry to reproduce, angels cannot reproduce, how is it that we who are intelligent beings believe in such things, angels with male reproductive organs?

The power of the serpent, the power of suggestion and indoctrination dulls our thinking, "Sons of God" represent our true nature as spiritual beings. When we fail to live as our true selves, we fall, we associate ourselves with menial, earthly things, physical objects, and things created, but the creeping crawling serpents which are by nature, base creatures, we elevate into gods, and demons. Man has the power to imbue upon inanimate matter the power of life. It is in our own minds that we create fear, for the spirit of fear does not originate with God. These lowly earthly thoughts of things formed in our minds are the **daughters of man. False thoughts** solidified as the gospel by the spiritual sons of God **are the giants.** In their minds, distorted truth becomes immoveable and grand like giants. These are the giants formed on the earth by man's unnatural thoughts and relationships with created things.

    Demons are the result of developed coping mechanisms, stop carrying pain and hurt and the demons will flee. You give hurtful memories the power to rule you only for as long as you decide to be ruled by the memories. The longer we carry hurt, the more powerful hurt becomes, just as a child is nourished from an embryo into an adult, we nourish thought seed into the power that rules over us. We create false images when we are unable to live as our true selves, we are creators, create life for yourselves and let their demons rule over those who created them.

    Remember, he was a liar from the beginning, when a liar speaks, everything he speaks is a lie. Adam and Eve lied on a snake that could not speak, God cursed

Adam and Eve, but the snake kept on crawling. Religion gave the snake legs, the ability to speak and walk upright like a man and in its final form, ruler of man and rival to God. He was a liar from the beginning, but not to those who have imbued him with their own authority... Stop giving people and things the authority to rule over you, none should rule you but God. You have the power to release or to hold captive everything that hurts you. ***You are the Master...***

God told Cain; you must rule over it. Did God not know that Adam had fallen over the very same serpent He is telling Cain to rule? Had not sin entered the world through Adam and man now subject to sin? How could God expect for Cain to rule and master what we all have been told we are subject to? The man who knows God does not know weakness, only you can destroy your demons, they are uniquely yours... The word demon comes not from the Old Testament but from the Greeks, look at the etymology of the word demon; *Old English demon, from Latin daemon, from Greek daimōn* **'deity, genius**. By definition, you have made your serpent into a deity, and a god when you fail to rule over it.

Cain could rule it for it was not his God, it was what Adam ate that changed his own life. If your religion keeps you from believing this, prayerfully read Ezekiel 18. Adam sinned because he wanted to sin, not because something overpowered him. Like Adam we sin because we want to sin, in fact we have created a religion which tells us that the serpent made us do it. Take responsibility for your own life and be successful; Take Up Your Cross and Follow Christ Who Lives In You. Hold on to Christ, not the religion of the serpent. God created man in His Image and man has the authority to create other gods, giving new meaning to, "Choose this day whom you will serve; the created gods of man or the Creator of All. Choose... Man has authority to Choose with his mind what exists in his world.

The World is Mental...

When two people come together in a relationship without first acknowledging or at least, being aware of the psychological effects of their own childhood trauma, they create the offspring of trauma, **daughters of men**. It is like the perpetrator who has long passed away, yet lives. This because the mental environment of the parents; they are functioning in normalized disfunction, they physically create a human being who shares their Genetic or Psychogenic DNA of abuse. Mental and physical abuse can be transferred from one generation to the next until the so called "curse is reversed" and the Demon Destroyed. This curse and its demons are not rulers of you, but you've been taught that there is a force other than God greater than you. On the contrary, you are ruler over every thought you hold in your mind, get it... hold in your mind. Demons are but haunting memories held captive by the mind.

Remember this, when the demon possessed man was confronted by Jesus, since the demons knew the truth, they asked Him not to destroy them; the lie is destroyed by the truth. To hold on to the lie, we must create a fallen world forged by abnormal thoughts, actions and false perceptions of ourselves and others. These unnatural thoughts cause us to create distorted relationships with others, seeing in them what lives in us, we project our demons on them, not knowing that we See in others what we first See in ourselves. 90% of our physical world comes from our own perception. Remember, The World Is Mental. We've been taught about demons and devils, but what if our demons are inherited? What if we give birth to our demons and feed and nurture them in the proper environment until they are old enough to break away and create their own kingdom of dystopia.

Mothers teach their little girls to be protective of their bodies for fear of arousing the pedophilia desire of uncle James, but Uncle James did not assault you mom, he loves his niece, why create this fear in your child and call it protection. The victim who was sexually assaulted when only a child was you, why victimize your daughter and expose her to the same hand that touched you? Since the little girl doesn't fully understand the psychology behind her mother's protection the opposite effect is imposed. She is ashamed of her body and feels ugly until one day the wrong woman makes her feel beautiful, the love she never had from a man. Mommy told me that men were bad, I couldn't separate the two. Mommy, because of you, I've never liked men. What do you mean because of me? Baby, I've never taught you to distrust men. Wait... did I?

Mommy, we've been hypnotized... This, the animal magnetism shared between parent and child.

If there are demons in church, they are the people who are living with unresolved childhood nightmares. Don't be a victim of this superstitious belief, nothing can possess you unless you possess it. God gave you that power and if God doesn't take over your mind and body without your consent, then neither can anything else have power over you unless you create it with the Creative Power of Your Mind.

The average adult doesn't know their childhood pain until they hurt people in their own adult lives. We often hurt those closest to us and do not understand the source of our own pains. Two people agreeing to take part in a relationship without first addressing Cognitive Distortions of the Mind. These distortions of life come not from outside one's home but from within. We appear to smile on the outside while there is a crying child held captive on the inside. When I hurt you, it is not the person I want to be that is committing the act but the subconscious child in me who is in poverty and distress because at 17, his mother was forced to be a woman. *"The Church would not accept this behavior, I'm a Pastor and my own household is out of order, I had to put her out, she got pregnant out of wedlock!"*

YOU'VE BEEN HYPNOTIZED

Just like God is quick to expel sin, I too must expel my own child! But wait, does not the church teach forgiveness and love? Haven't you ever read about child sacrifice? I had to sacrifice my child to God to remove the sin of her youth and I condemned all the children she carried in her womb to perpetual poverty and strife. Look at how her children were raised, they don't know the meaning of fidelity, all of them became possessed by the spirit of lust, infidelity, perversion, anger, and bitterness. Yes, the hand who touched her has impressed upon her children, psychological instability, but it's ok in this world to normalize disfunction, her children blend in with the rest of the world. We all have psychological challenges, normalized by those who want you to be who they need you to be.

For their mother sang in that same choir. What Choir? Sing the Song Annie Mae! And you better not make us look bad before the congregation; the church thinks she got pregnant by the neighbor's son...

Dear 1st Lady,

Silence Implies Consent.

THE ALCHEMIST

The Alchemist is getting ready to work on your mind to transform you; Watch this... *When the people went out of their way to make her sad, she put in the work to make them laugh. They hated her because like a mirror, she reflected them. She could not be broken!*

There was no bad in her, her religious parents could not preach it into her, and there was none for her blind boyfriend to beat out of her; the world didn't give it and the world couldn't take it away. At her funeral, the people said the entire church was full, there was standing room only. In the midst of their grief and pain, every eye wet from tears, no one could believe she was gone! Then suddenly, there was a rumbling but peaceful, a rush of air but calm, and their tears dried up, the preacher stop preaching and in came the feeling of a silence. Although silent, the people heard a laugh and a voice said, "Well done my good and faithful child, I AM the meaning of your joy will be complete." I am the living testimony, those who say they love Me, should first get to know Me. I didn't come into the world to condemn the world, but they are condemned already, those who do not Love.

She came to save them, but they hated her. May they live in the world they created without her. God confronted them with love but they desired hate. She was oppressed and afflicted, yet she did not open her mouth. Like a lamb led to the slaughter and like a sheep silent before her shearers, she did not open her mouth against those who persecuted her. She was taken away because of oppression and judgment; and who considered her fate? They made her grave with the wicked and with a rich man at her death. Her parents didn't know that she was already born again. At her death, is when she began to live in them, it was not she who lived but Christ, she was alive, but they were dead without her. He forgave them... It was he who they persecuted. He is the Son of Man who makes them alive, without this Son in Man, Man would live dead.
This is deep...

He came eating and drinking, in the form of a woman and her religious parents said, "Here is a glutton and a drunkard, a friend of sinners; how could she get pregnant out of wedlock? But wisdom is proved right by her deeds." He brought joy to drunkards, they were in pain, why else did they drink so much? They were gluttons because they could not be satisfied, for what they craved, The Top Chef could not create. Yet the Lord was pleased to crush her, and we will see her seed, He will prolong her days, and by His hand, the Lord's pleasure will be accomplished, she is alive today in those who knew and loved her. Her crucifixion has caused her to be in places she would have never been, she lives on at the wonderful age of 50 now, death gave her life. When you lie down at night at the end of your most difficult days with a smile on your face, she is lying down beside you.

    She is the representation of what great minds have pondered for centuries; how to transform base metals into precious metals. We can't even begin to understand what makes bitter lemons sweet... When someone offers you bitter fruit, there is no power in the fruit itself. Watch this... It is not what enters a man that makes him corrupt it is when the man receives the fruit and processes it internally that the Self is revealed. The fruit that we share reflects the life that lives within. The fruit only represents the opportunity for the man to be made known. She will teach you if you are ready to learn. Her friends know her as Ella, I call her, "The Alchemist", her laugh will transform you... She was misunderstood since times long ago; the Egyptians called her Isis, the Greeks Sophia, the Christians call her Mary, from the outside looking in, Wisdom was her name.

Now let me tell you about **Ella...**

They say Ella committed suicide; I say those who were already dead killed her. Have you ever met someone who when they laughed, everyone laughed without knowing what was funny? The way she laughed, was the definition of funny. Her laugh was both audibly and viscerally infectious, what made her laugh unique was that you could feel the happiness in her. Her laugh was the life that lived inside of her and if you were one of the few lucky ones to have met her, she would live in you forever.

Not everyone understands what means, "the spirit of joy", it gets in you, and it infects you and for the sake of other people's joy, even when you're crying inside, you never let them see your pain. It was like she could feel your pain and do something funny to take it away. Now that I think back, she was put on earth with the ability to absorb the pain and suffering of the world, transform it and give you a part of herself in return. She had a supernatural ability, sort of like a superhero who could transform negative energy into positive energy. Why do people like her die so young? It's as if they come to earth, touch the select, deliver their message, and poof, their gone. It doesn't take long to give from what is so plentiful, it was overflowing and running over around the edges, everyone who ever met her, still drinks from her cup. Even her birth was strange, she wasn't from here, America I mean. She was a mixture of them both, her father didn't understand the role he played though.

Before she appeared on earth, she was born in him, he went on a journey to Germany to plant his seed, it's amazing the power of Joy! It moves you! Even when you don't understand the reason for the journey, you must move.

Once she came to him, he was only a vessel, the Army didn't call him, it was Ella's mother whose voice he heard. The entire world is mental, open your eyes and you will feel what you cannot hear. He delivered them both to the messenger, she was waiting for them when they came. The whole story is understood now, no wonder Ella's father called her mom, maybe she was the magician moving the pieces, no, she was only a pawn, Ella was the star of this show. Soon after Ella's birth, her father having played his part, he drifted back into her memory, just as she summoned him, she caused him to return, he was most insignificant. Now when someone gives you something or when we receive a favor from someone, it is often realized that the debt and price that our misfortune incurs is never paid. Ella and her mother, now abandoned by their father and husband, were sold in a sense to religious bondage to Mother Pearl, so heavenly bound to be any earthly good, all who enter must do so through Mrs. Pearl.

    Mrs. Pearl was a religious person, and to live in her house, you had to live a life pleasing to God as defined by Mrs. Pearl's religious doctrines. Ella's mother had been subjected to this chain of unfortunate situations and trials because of her life of sin and God was punishing her for what she had done, that's why her husband abandoned her with child. Why else would such a thing happen unless God was dissatisfied with her life. She gave up the bad habits which were the cause of her ills and accepted the denomination of Mother Pearl.

Ella's mother had been converted to these new religious beliefs even before she was able to speak fluent English, a true testimony! She went on and became gainfully employed, saved enough money and she and Ella were able to move into their own home to where she carried these liberating religious beliefs. She understood that when a person disobeys God, their lives will be filled with doom, misfortune, and punishment, since all that she experienced was because of God's displeasure with her; she was serving a God who lacked compassion and did not allow children to make mistakes. The God who gave his own son is the same one who lacks compassion and since God deals with his subjects this way, the parent who spares the rod ruins the child and prevents entrance into Mrs. Pearls heaven.

Ella's mother rarely spared the rod as Ella was growing up, displaying the strong arm of God per her religious doctrine. Living in low-income housing Ella's mother believed that their only hope for success was to follow the letter of the word to shew evil and live, even if this required harsh treatment of those you love, this was pleasing to God when he would see that a parent could turn her back on a child who is yet learning and finding the way that she should go. The word says "raise a child" for a reason. It's amazing that God would tell his children to do what He is not willing to do, tolerate learning with love. There was a time when Ella was only 10 years old, she was physically punished by her mother in a harsh way. Although Ella's skin eventually mended and the wounds closed, I don't believe Ella ever recovered emotionally from the mental scars she received for doing something common for a 10-year-old.

One day as Ella was attempting to surprise her sleeping mother with a Mother's Day breakfast, she wasted half the pancake mix on the floor and her mother became infuriated beyond belief. Not because of the wasted food but because she told Ella never to bring pagan rituals into her house again. Now, by the time Ella was 10, she stood eye to eye with her mother, so when it was time for her to be punished, she would have Ella strip down to her under clothes and lay on her stomach (on the bed) with her arms and legs spread out and she would beat her! With whatever weapon she could get her hands on, she would use it. Yes, weapon because to bring such a thing into her home was an act of the enemy.

    She beat the enemy with the weapon of righteousness. She would make Ella take off her clothes... Let's take a closer look at these acts of abuse by Ella's mother and let's undress her. She was the one suffering from deep psychological trauma, at this point Ella was not yet traumatized, she still had the joy of an innocent child, she had not yet been broken, it was her mother who was broken. We can identify her brokenness by her physical acts. Who was she stripping? It was a child, but it wasn't Ella. She was undressing someone, but it wasn't the little girl she loved, she was undressing someone else, someone she hated. We shall call Ella's mother Hilda, for it was young Hilda she hated.

    Who is Hilda? Hilda was the little German girl who learned how to move like a woman at only 12 years of age and she hated her mother for it. Hilda never liked herself and her mother made her this way. Hilda's stepdad would have his way with her. When Hilda would tell her mother, Ella's grandmother, she would get stripped down to her underwear and the unspeakable would happen and then she would ask Hilda, is this what you wanted? You wanted this so much that you would lie on an innocent man? Now look at you! You're so ugly when you cry! Hilda's mother would always tell Hilda what an ugly person she was although she was a very beautiful girl with curly red hair.

    She was the eldest of her siblings and would be the first to get home from school, she would linger around at school for as long as she could trying to avoid Herr Hans (Mr. Hans) who instead of helping Hilda with her homework, helped himself with her (Hilda's mom worked in the evenings). She never felt clean, never felt pure, never felt like a beautiful little girl. When she looked in the mirror, as she was beating Ella one day, she saw little Hilda standing there with her hair cut off unevenly and scratches on her face and she broke the glass, she hated that image even until this day. Hilda developed faster than most of her peers because she was receiving a man. It didn't stop there for her, even her brothers joined in, well one brother in particular.

    Hilda had started to confide in her younger but eldest of her brothers for support and things between them became sexual as emotions led from sibling comfort to love. One day the youngest brother said he walked in on what looked like two adults in love; Hilda and her brother were wet with sweat. With so much practice, Hilda could move like a woman, a boy was no match for her. Herr Hans would smoke a cigarette after the abuse, a habit that Hilda had adopted. Before she learned to smoke, she would lie down and cry herself to sleep after the abuse. Sometimes, she would cry for no apparent reason, the world didn't know her pain, no wonder she lived the life she did.

    Have you ever cried, and no one cared? Have you ever asked God why he created you? Have you ever wanted to curse God and die? She used to ask God to take her life so many times, but Hilda kept right on living, and so did the pain.

    Maybe this is who I am, maybe I'm cursed, and if sex eases the pain, there is no wonder she had so many men in her small town, they helped her feel pretty! Concealing her pain, she learned to be the best; she could do it like no other. She became a sex goddess, and the men were but pawns on a chess board. Ella's father met Hilda this way, what should've been a one-night stand in a German town, poured over into the states, he had no clue how deep runs her pain, so he drifted away... When Hilda became a woman, nothing calmed her like a good cigarette, a habit she had all her life... What happened to Hans? No one knows but Hilda's brother was big for his age and very strong. He loved Hilda and the people say it was a terrible farming accident. The emotional scars of a child run deep and many of us turn to coping mechanisms to conceal the past.

Hilda loved sex and men loved her, but she did not love herself. She turned to drugs at one point in her life to hide the pain. The men in her life didn't know that they were just a means to an end. Hilda was trying to kill the crying red head within. Many of us know this redhead and many of us have our own vices. The more Ella matured; she reminded Hilda of herself. In a way she loved Ella in the sense that she didn't want her to experience the life she hated. She wanted Ella to live a Godly life and settle down with a good man from the church to which she had turned.

Ella was taller than her mother, had a smooth even complexion, mixed with African American and German, Ella was very pretty; those mixed babies are so pretty, and their hair is to die for. *Pay attention to this cycle.* Remember that Hilda's mother worked 2nd shift, so did Hilda. Not only are our lives regulated by a circadian rhythm, but our habits are also affected by impressions on our subconscious minds. The things we consciously think about, although disliked, we become. Remember that the evil in Hilda's life would take place at dusk during second shift. Many are the evils of single parents who must leave their children at home alone to make a living. There are countless teen mothers whose babies were conceived during an eight-hour evening shift when my mother leaves, come in from the back.

    At around 13 Ella became best friends with another mature little girl named Dena. Although they had known each other since elementary school they did not start to bond until middle school. As their friendship grew, they started to do everything together. Hilda seemed to approve of their friendship, since she had met Dena's parents. Although Hilda took notice that Dena was quite a developed and mature little girl, but most African American girls are more mature in certain areas and Dena was by far not an exception. Ella and Dena laughed about the time when Hilda asked Dena, "Are those cotton jeans or do you have cotton in your genes?"

However, Hilda approved of their friendship, and it gave Hilda a sense of security especially that Dena's home was not far from theirs and with one of the Witnesses from the Kingdom checking in from time to time, she felt that Ella would be safe at home alone.

They lived in a community of Witnesses in which Ella had taken an interest and this pleased Hilda. Ella and Dena did everything together and even met boys together without Hilda's knowledge. Ella met a young man in middle school, and they became boyfriend and girlfriend, this was typical puppy love and soon faded when Ella went off to high school since he was one grade behind her.

Things changed when Ella and Dena entered high school, they met different types of boys. They met big boys, short boys, tall boys, handsome boys and oh girl, he looks like a man-boy, I'm scared of him, but I hope he calls me... Boys, Boys, and don't your momma work 2nd shift boys! Girl, he lifts weights! I'm gonna do it! Do what? Only go on a date with him with a witness chaperone. There's no way I can be alone with him. Yeah right, I don't need anyone with me, I'm not going all the way and besides, my mother would kill me... You remember what she did to me for making pancakes, only God knows what she'd do if she caught us mixing batter in the bedroom... And then Ella would crack up laughing with her infectious laugh every time she tells a funny joke and that's why I miss her so...

Have you ever missed not just the person but their soul? That's how Dena described her emptiness when Ella's mother killed her best friend. Dena said as she thinks back, it didn't happen overnight, it started a long time ago. Over time, the girls grew closer and closer and just like innocent little girls, they shared everything, shoes, clothes, and stories. Dena and Ella became like sisters, I believe they lost their virginity together, so they said, but you know how girls tell stories. They both were good girls, although Dena was questionably developed for her age, even men would look twice sometimes.

They say she ate good, especially Sunday dinners, she naturally had what other people are paying for these days, maybe it really is the cornbread. Second thought, it may have been the collard greens, and blackeye peas, you know how only your momma could make them with fatback and a little okra to taste and don't forget the pepper for a little attitude on the side...

Yeah, it was the food, a lot of Black girls have that leg and hip problem, it's their favorite part of the chicken if you know what he likes, cook it for him! Oh, how we love a woman who can... Cook! If you would see her today, you would say, "Yeah, it's definitely the cornbread!"

Love Could Never Love You...

Hilda's friend and neighbor was excommunicated from the Kingdom because she too could cook... Fried chicken thighs were her specialty, if thighs were your thing, you couldn't resist hers. It's amazing how big chicken thighs were back then. The sisters said she invited a male friend over and shared the recipe with him and he never went back home, he said his mother never cooked thighs like hers. It was evident that the kingdom didn't approve of her giving her recipe away so soon, even though they did get married shortly after, fornication was unforgiveable once found out. However, many single women have their private devices, and are still in the church... Burning psychologically with sexual desires can be hidden but which is worst? Fornication or judgement? Who are we to judge?

Many children born in religious households never recognize abuse until years later when they become the abuser. I've seen this firsthand, brothers and sisters in rigid religious homes fathering and mothering children, but some stories are best untold. There are people in your family who have turned to devices to quiet a crying baby, Aunt Josephine didn't want to be a drug addict, the drugs kept her from destroying the good church family, my own mother was a sacrifice! Secrets she took to the grave, saved the family. A lot of Uncle Joe's babies have been buried in the Church's cemetery... We owe a debt to all the men and women who never told the truth.

Can we judge so-called religious people so harshly as to think that they are different from those who don't consider themselves religious at all?

Aren't we all to some degree indoctrinated and affected by the past which causes the creation of doctrines, laws and even commandments to guide our households? Don't we indoctrinate our children with so-called lessons from our past to protect them? Was that who my mother was? Was she truly a sacrifice, was she abused as a child and the life she lived in response to the pain she carried or the secrets she bore? Or is this the image that I must form of her so that I may preserve my sanity? Or do I just need to paint a positive picture of her, viewing her as a victim so that I can function properly in the face of all the negative emotions formed as I experienced the life she lived? What would happen to a child who had to come to the realization that the one he should look up to and respect as parent was just like a prostitute on the street? Who would he cling to and bond with? Yeah but, prostitutes are different right? They do it in back alleys, empty houses and sleezy motels, they are the worst. Ladies on the other hand, do it in their homes and 5-star hotels, they are different, no matter how many uncles, cousins, and stepdads their children knew.

What then happens to the respect a son should have for his mother? What happens to the little girl who looks up to her father and it is he who got her pregnant for the second time? It is devastating psychologically when those to whom a child must bond, the closest members of the tribe, become the perpetrators of sexual, mental, or physical abuse. The very person from whom protection is sought, comes trauma. With whom then does that child identify? The child creates a negative identity not of the perpetrator but of him or herself. To identify positively with mother and father is to develop a positive image of self, the self is representative of the immediate group. When that bond is broken, the child is unable to comprehend fault with the parent but instead turns against themselves. When momma and daddy don't love the child, the child forms a negative identity, something is wrong with me, not the group. Therefore, I become less so that the perpetrator becomes more until I hate myself and when I find someone who loves me, it is that person I then abuse...

The self I hate, I kill and who I become, I create so that I do not have to disassociate myself from the group. I create a person who becomes numb to the ills of the group so that I may be accepted.

To do this, I must destroy my self-image because I need my mother to be good, although she causes me pain. Ella became a coal walker, numb to the pain. After having multiple conversations with herself, "I'm okay," "I'm beautiful," "I'm okay," "I'm OKAY! No, I'm not okay, my mom hates me, I must not be okay. Why would she hate me if I was okay? My human nature makes it difficult for me to be okay when you are not... A child doesn't know how to do this, and for an adult to detach, it is extremely difficult, the child must become someone else, and the adult will never be the same...

Why is it that we can't see death until it is physical? To some degree, don't we all need a type of delusion, whether its religious indoctrination or mental images we form of people so that they become who we need them to become so that we become who we want to become? We need people to be who we need them to be for our own survival, even if it means recreating them for our own sanity. Who would you be without negative experiences, who would you be without adversities? Most people think that they would be better off in life had it not been for the negative experiences and circumstances of life. But is that totally true? The entire world has been affected by adversity and wickedness and in response have created dogmas, myths and to some degree, even family cults which propagate their own survival and perpetuate their brand and name.

In response to what we call wickedness and misfortune, lessons learned have resulted in family dynamics and these dynamics identify us as a part of one group, but separate us from another, the reason for last names. We are this or that family, and we don't live like those across town, little girls in this house don't wear skirts to the movies, not because mother and father are strict but because we love you and these are our rules... Our rules are for protection, because as parents, we have knowledge of evils that our children do not, even something as innocent as a first date at the movies, no ma'am, we don't wear that to the movies, and your father and I will also be there, two rows away! Yes, all of us have been affected by evils, we would not know our true selves if it were not for so called evils of the world or wickedness.

    So don't be so quick to judge the religious, we are all in some form, delusional. It is in the vein of protection that we keep our children from certain things. So don't judge those who have created certain holy spaces of protection called commandments, but instead, be thankful if you have never been abused. Isn't it wise to protect children from pain and trauma? Especially those situations which have been a hindrance in our own paths. If the Adam and Eve story is the foundation of your religious beliefs, do you realize that you would not have a savior, or even a religion had it not been for deceit, disobedience and lies, it would be difficult at best to understand worship if not first, the fall. There would be no worship of God if not for disobedience. Think about that, do we even know good without evil? Even the savior of the world had to have the knowledge of evil so that the world could be saved.

Ella the Alchemist is a 2-story story, just as Ella had to see joy in painful places; in essence make brick without straw, we all must take base metals, we all must take pain and transform the negative into life, or we would live in the death that kills us. For without delusion, we would see things as they are and most of us rather not see... Therefore, we create realities for ourselves, he who does not do this would not be alive, he would live in another man's world. That's why they grow up so quickly, the child became the sacrifice. Then you see adults doing childish things... That's why she could move like a woman... Her youth was stolen!

Back to the story, although this was painful for Hilda, she never again spoke to her friend. Hilda had the ability to be cold with a turn of a switch. She had done this since a child, you must understand that all of us have coping mechanisms we turn on and off. All of us live in some sort of deception, or invented world where alter egos rule. We could not lead healthy lives without delusion, some delusion is considered as healthy if it keeps you sane and focused on success. When a person says, "I don't need you!" Believe them, they are preparing and conditioning their minds to live without you. Soon you will see that they are becoming distant from you, although at home with you, they are far from you, look at Hilda's face, her house is so empty, but her loyalty was to Jehovah and not to her worldly friend because Jesus didn't hang with people like that...

In fact, the church wouldn't have known about the relationship had it not been for Hilda. She knew that her friend wanted to marry the guy, but they got weak one time and gave in to each other and Hilda reported it as if they willfully and daily engaged in premarital sex. Is it so easy for God to give up on us? Why even go to church if you are already condemned? However, her friend could never belong to another man-made Kingdom Hall again. Another soul lost?

Meanwhile, Dena and Ella were continuing to grow and not only in size but their desire for boys also grew and Ella ran into Jason Hook from middle school. He had matured and was still interested in Ella, and she was interested in him. It did not take long for him to figure out that her mom worked in the evenings and that she was alone most of the time. He became friends with Dena to get closer to Ella, you know how that works, get the friend to talk to her about me. Jason Hook's plan worked, he even started showing up in the girl's neighborhood unannounced, and almost everywhere he knew the girls would be without their parents. Jason understood the power of investing time, he was with Ella every chance he got. He eventually talked Ella into letting him come over, and he never came over without a gift. He would always tell her how beautiful she was and how he just could not get enough of her. She started wearing his starter jacket to school, his idea of course, Mr. Hook wanted to stay not just on Ella's mind but even on her body too.

    It was not long before his plan succeeded, and he and Ella had intercourse. It seemed as if Hilda had a knack for detecting fornication, a sort of 6th sense. One day while doing laundry, she noticed spots of blood in Ella's underwear, and she nearly blew her top! Hilda was a very loyal saint, and she immediately took this matter to the elders.

The elders explained that although Ella had not been baptized and could not be disfellowshipped she would be considered bad association if her behavior continued, Ella was 16 years old. Hilda thought about what the elders said, but this was her only child. Hilda's house was empty, and life had caused her heart to run cold, although she had lost a best friend, and the only relative close to her was Ella, there was only one decision for her to make, she put Ella, now only 16 years old out of the house and into the arms of Jason Hook. His family accepted and embraced her as a child who needed love and guidance. After 3 months with Jason's family, Ella returned home, but little did Hilda know that children do childish things and when they are abandoned without intelligent decision-making skills, they make even worse decisions, sort of like Hilda's own childhood when she turned to her brother for comfort and gratification.

Well, when Ella returned home, she didn't return alone. Once Hilda realized that Ella had become pregnant, she was really enraged and put Ella out again but by this time, Jason was working and wanted a family with Ella, so they moved in together to be the perfect family with a story to tell. Well, everything didn't go as planned, Jason was very controlling, and what he said was the law, especially since even Ella's own mother didn't want her. Shortly after moving in together, Jason became more and more controlling, when he wanted to have sex, it didn't matter if she wanted to or was ready or not, he would make her. Jason had always been a bully in school, but Ella ignored the signs because she loved Jason, and his family had plenty of money. He seemed to think more of himself than anyone else because of his family's status. There were times when Ella wanted to leave Jason, but Hilda had long since stopped communicating with her, it was as if the two were dead to one another.

    There was no turning back for them, Ella was living the life of a heathen, and a heathen has no place in the church. This caused Ella to cling even more to the only man who had ever loved her. He did love her... right? At least he was there for her, she never heard from her dad again, she knew he didn't care.

Although Jason was controlling and at times abusive, Ella married him. Ella gave birth to a handsome little boy who Hilda just could not resist and with Jason and Ella's marriage, it was permissible for Hilda to associate with her again and with her grandchild. Ella didn't talk to Hilda about what was going on with Jason behind closed doors, she only spoke to her friend Dena about the abuse. She wanted to talk to her mother, but she knew that she would lose her again, since divorce was not permissible without proof of infidelity. Dena knew that Jason had given her a few looks when Ella's back was turned as if he wanted something from her but, there was no true proof of anything except abuse. There were a few times that Ella had to wear shades to work to cover black eyes. Once Jason beat her for not cooking a meal the way he liked it and another time for getting mud on the rims of his car.

Dena would often tell Ella to leave him, but Ella wanted to be loved and besides, she wanted her son to have a father that she did not. Eventually Ella stopped telling Dena about the abuse and the two became distant. The abuse went on for several years and it seemed as if Ella had lost her soul, even her self-identity, she became who Jason said she could be. After Jason nearly took her life, Ella finally got the courage to leave him, but she couldn't stand being alone, although dysfunctional, she had a family with Jason, and all she ever wanted was to be loved.

Ella soon met a new man, someone very different from Jason, someone who treated her son like his own. This is what Ella wanted all her life and she found it in Donnie. The two married soon after they started dating and Ella became pregnant with a beautiful baby girl, who was the joy of Ella's life. Soon, Ella and Donnie's relationship changed, they started to yell at each other and call each other dirty names. Ella was with a new man, but in an old relationship...

Dena said she remembered once when Ella cried and said no one could ever love me! It's me! My daddy left me, and no man could ever love me! My own mother didn't even want me. One night after a heated argument, Donnie left home and stayed out all night. Ella took her life that night, she shot herself in the head with Donnie's gun! When Ella died, she had a 5-month-old baby girl, and a 7-year-old son. Ella was only 23...

YOU TOUCHED ME, BUT HURT MY CHILD

Times have surely changed, back then, people had morals and values, we lived holy lives. How did she learn of such a thing in the 50's? Well sir, distortions most often start at home. As the pious wife sleeps with her eyes open, it happens in her own household, she just kept own singing in the choir. We are a religious family; all my kids go to church. I know lady and I understand; thus, sleeping is even easier, for we see demons in the house when we are awake. For your own life was not what it seemed, the same hand that touched her, you also knew. He was from your household; your womb gave birth to him. What do you mean, my womb gave birth to him? Well maybe or maybe not physically but look at the environment your psychosomatic blindness created.

C'mon, you saw him, you saw how he looked at her in church. He would come over every Sunday for dinner, she was his favorite niece, he favored her. Why else has she developed so fast? She doesn't even look her age; he wouldn't let her be a child. The child in her was put to death, but was resurrected in all her many intimate relationships, they say she laid down with at least 30 different men and her daughter is haunted by all of them... What does it mean to become spiritually dead? Physical pleasure and emotional connection of the orgasm, the two become one, the I or Ego is lost; culminant of the two at the highest point of their affection. Culminant is a word to describe an astronaut's ascent into space, to reach the highest point, the meridian or in Traditional Chinese medicine, the Jing-luo or Meridian points.

We view sex as a physical act, in fact, according to the etymology of the word orgasm, it refers to the physical act of the swelling of the male or female sexual organ at the highest point of excitement, but this physical transition does not capture what is happening emotionally and spiritually.

In TCM, Traditional Chinese Medicine, healing takes place through certain points on the body known as Meridian Points or Jing-Luo, which are activated or stimulated to affect Qi. Pronounced Chee, defined in the most basic sense of the word Vital Life Force. In understanding Qi, there is a physical substance and then there is what I want you to pay attention to, so you will understand the spiritual and psychological meaning of sex. The activation of these meridian points by the skilled therapist of acupuncture is like what takes place during every sexual exchange we have, there is a spiritual and a physical exchange. We become one with each sexual partner we have, an amalgamation of all our encounters here on earth. No wonder Jesus asked the woman, "where is your husband?" We all have many husbands and wives, once virginity is lost, it can never be regained. Man, she's a virgin and I'm going to tear that up when I get some. He got some and left her alone, abandoned, and defiled, to live a life long adulterous life.

She was his wife, every encounter after him was adultery... Man he really did tear her up, left that little innocent child to die...

Concerning Qi, we are interested in the invisible rather than the physical, the vital energy itself which flows through our bodies when the fluid of intercourse leaves one body and enters another... Have you noticed the scent of sex; the physical implication of the intertwining of spirits, The Spiritual Orgasm? What happens when he gets up, cleans himself off and leaves you alone, dirty, and empty? What it takes him minutes to clean off, it takes you a lifetime to repair. I've been in a relationship with you and saw his hands all over your body, I knew you were not my wife, everything you did was in response to him. The woman I hurt, has become another man's wife. Later in life, I see her again in a totally different woman with the same hurt from another man's hands; the woman I scarred comes back to me, we pass her around so that all our boys can get some. This is Qi, the Vital Life Force that is damaged when we, "yeah girl, I gave him some." Some? No sweety, you gave him all, you gave so much away, until you have nothing else to give. Woman after woman, we take some from.

The woman I first fell in Love with was emptied when she were just a child and her daddy abandoned her. Why do we fall, as in "fall in love"? This is the attitude we take when we don't understand what is happening spiritually. The entire race has fallen because sex has become a physical act... Have you ever loved someone who has been damaged by their past? A woman I once loved, was scarred by what she heard her mother and Mr. Johnson doing. She would lie in bed crying as her mother was trying to get the rent paid. Mr. Johnson paid the rent and got a little bit, Mr. Jackson got a little bit, and so did Mr. McCain. I wanted to kill Mr. McCain myself after she told me that her mother was in the kitchen getting high with him. The only time he would come over was during the night. She said she had a gun aimed at him one night as Mr. McCain and her mother were sitting down smoking at the kitchen table. No wonder she couldn't love me, the Hands that touched the mother, caused her child to die. Her mother, abandoned and abused as a child, all her life she wanted her father to care for her like he cared for the people at church, he wouldn't even step foot in her house, was he too holy to sit with sinners?

No, his guilt would not let him in, he heard about what his daughter had become and couldn't face the offspring of his own ignorance.

I remember she told me how her mother stood in the cold looking through the living room window as the rest of the family opened Christmas presents. Many of us have daughters like this, children left behind... Who will pick up the pieces? Who will love enough to see through that outer garment, those "Fig Leaves" to go back and rescue the inner child. I'm hurting inside and all I ever wanted was Love... She said since she didn't understand

Qi, she learned how to "Make Love" get it? She knew how to create a physical feeling in the bedroom. She made it feel like heaven! Have you ever been with someone who knows how to make the bedroom feel like heaven? That person seems as if s/he could package it up and sell it! Get down to the root of their skill, ask them from where their talent comes? And then again, some lie in the bed every night with a dead man or woman and don't even know it. You knew she was dead; she's not moving but all you wanted was a feeling, you didn't even stop to figure out what makes her happy or why she's sad. So, every day, we interact and lie down with a dead person, a person who is full of dis-ease Get it, disease?

    In TCM, the practitioner is attempting to bring the body, mind, and spirit into harmony by activating Meridian Points. Pay attention to this, you've heard it before. Since we are talking about Hands that Prey, you've heard that the Son and The Father are One. In Qi, the idea is that the Mind, Body, and Spirit must be in Harmony, (The Holy Trinity) for the individual to be whole. Well, when a person is in a dis-eased state, this means that somehow, there is interference in the body, a foreign agent has entered the body; the 3 are no longer in agreement. Think of the individual body and every living thing as an interconnected and interdependent System. When dis-ease is in the body, the system of things will be disturbed. We make and receive spiritual deposits to and from one another with every interaction we have, knowingly and unknowingly. How can a person be whole when the perception of their own nature has been stained? When the son doesn't know the father, he walks around in darkness. How can my woman expect me to recognize her pain when I too hear a child crying in the dark? Baby, I can't recognize your hurt, because I'm depending on you to heal me. You are the closest I've ever been to a mother, mine, I never knew. All I've ever known was the physical act...

Have you ever been in love with a person who was the victim of abuse and couldn't figure out why that person wouldn't or couldn't let you love them?

Let me tell you a story... I know this brother; we'll say his name is Strong. Strong told me a story about him and his wife and some problems they had. He said he loved that woman like a man could only love his mother, but for some reason, she didn't recognize it; we'll call her Celeste, she was heavenly. Celeste and Strong would argue and fight like every couple does, right? Every couple argue, fuss and curse each other out right? And then have passionate make up sex. Strong said when they would have the worst fights, Celeste would turn the bedroom into heaven that night. They wouldn't speak for a few days but when they make up, Celeste knows what to do, she's "all the way turned on" after an argument, it's like she's someone else after a "good" fight! This is normal right, every couple has make-up sex? You don't know the meaning of Make-Up sex until it's against your will...

Strong said he believes the reason he started beating Celeste is because he figured she liked it, she didn't know how to talk or express herself unless they were fighting, then they would connect, it was like they made a spiritual connection after a fight. Strong said, it was like she functioned better in chaos rather than peace. One day when they got into one of their fights, it almost went too far when an image flashed in Strong's mind of him strangling her to death; sometimes we wish we could strangle our pain... He said he didn't know what came over him, it was like the two of them caused a presence of another being to enter the house, he wanted to kill the woman he loved, but something stopped him.

He had knocked Celeste to the floor, and she was lying there in the fetal position crying uncontrollably and he saw an image of a little girl and then he saw his own mother lying on that floor... Well, later that night as they were lying in bed, Celeste with a bruise on her face, and emptiness for a heart, Strong tired and sobering up, he had a few shots of bourbon after the fight. As Strong lied in the bed, half asleep and half awake, drifting in and out of consciousness, in a state of betweenness, the room got very quiet and still, he couldn't hear a thing. At that very moment, he felt a breeze, a light, warm breeze, and an image appeared in the room. It was Celeste's deceased mother, and Strong couldn't move, "he was weak" with fear.

She floated over and sat on his side of the bed, he said he saw an image, but he literally saw the imprint from her, the weight of her soul on his bed. Soon the image disappeared, but the impression remained, and he heard the voice of Celeste's mother. Her voice shook him, it felt as if she were speaking from deep within his own soul. She had come to him from beyond the grave, a place of brokenness was her home. She started to talk to him about her pain that she suffered, the pain of being the oldest child growing up in the 50's and having to take care of her younger brothers and sisters in a strict religious household where the mother had no voice, and her stepfather ruled, when there was a decision to be made, his word was final. She told him of a time when her stepfather would put sawdust in front of the doors and write his name in it so he would know if she left the house while he was away. He put the fear of God in the entire household.

He was the deacon in the church, and believed that we are all sinners and that there is no good in any of us and since he was a victim of sin, he didn't want sin in his house, coming in or going out... Celeste's mother told Strong, I know you think you're getting ready to have sex with my daughter but not tonight, tonight, you're getting ready to make love to me! Before you penetrate my daughter again, you call what you are doing to her making love, I call it rape! I'm going to show you what it's really like to make love to a dead woman! Strong said he was frozen and couldn't move. This woman had the strength of three men. She pulled his underwear to the side and had her way with him. As he was lying there behind her, he didn't know that she was crying because her back was turned to him, all he was thinking about was what he was thinking about. Halfway through she stopped crying and started performing, she knew how to turn it on and turn it off, she had to do this because he told her that he would kill me if she ever told what was going on. Listen to me Strong, I didn't listen to my daughter when she told me what he was doing to her, all I wanted was a happy home, even if it meant sacrificing one of my own children. I couldn't make him stay but my daughter did, she could always use those big hips. I figured if Celeste made him happy, I would have him, he would have Celeste and she would get over it... I did, didn't I?

My stepfather would put sawdust in front of the doors to make sure no other man entered his house...

You know about those hips Strong; you fell in love with those hips, all you do is objectify women! Don't you sit there and judge me, you don't love my daughter, you don't even know my daughter, the person she was, died a long time ago and you are too weak to give her life. Hell, she doesn't realize she married a dead man. Me and my husband killed Celeste, and your mother killed you, didn't she? You're nothing but a little boy in a man's body, you were probably raped yourself. Look at you, crying like a little chump. You were raped weren't you Strong? Strong, Strong! "Wake up man, wake up," you're drifting away...

Celeste said, "I almost killed a man... Yes, I spoke to her too, both were my friends... You wouldn't believe what she told me. I haven't been able to get in touch with Celeste to get the rest of the details, but when I do, I'll tell you her story, how she almost killed a man.

Have you ever laid awake at night and couldn't sleep because you heard demon screams of passion coming from the room of the only woman you ever loved at 12 years old? Have you ever even heard a demon scream? No, those were not demons, she was crying out for the pastor; the father who sacrificed her so that he could live.

Like prison bars...

Before this chapter ends, I must make mention of a young man with whom I had the pleasure of coaching and mentoring through a rough period of his life. This young man was in prison for a violent act, a crime of passion which landed him behind bars. His real name is Jericho, but he wanted me to call him Da' Feat because his real name was no longer significant, for the person he used to be was already dead and the person who now lives was only a fragment of who he once was.

    I remember telling him a story of my own life so that I might relate to his pain and PTSD by sharing with him the trauma I experienced in Desert Storm, The Liberation of Kuwait. It was after finally having a breakthrough moment with him that I realized how much we had in common. Although my enlistment was voluntary and his was not, he also experienced a traumatic incident which caused him to endure psychological and physical stress. He had endured sexual abuse, not by strange unfamiliar hands, but by the hands of his mother. He grew up fighting, well not physically but he had psychological battles in his own mind. What makes a child so angry, this young man was only 19 years old locked up in prison. He opened up to me and expressed his pain. He started with a question. He asked me, have you ever disrespected your mother? Do you know what it feels like to love your mother, I mean really love your mother so much that you couldn't tolerate being separated from her?

There were times when my mother would leave me home, I would experience separation anxiety, I've been in relationship after relationship, I still can't stand to be alone. Sounds familiar?

My mind never stops, it's never quiet, the impulse is overwhelming, it's like she is alive in me, one after another, I had 22 of them before I turned 18 and that still wasn't enough. I knew how to get them but couldn't understand what was needed to keep them, she was never home. I injured so many of them, they were only victims of my pain. Da' Feat said to me, "brother you don't understand what this sexual trauma did to me", so don't speak to me about the church when she went every Sunday without fail. In fact, the reason he beat her so badly is because she embarrassed him in front of the church. I'm going to beat the devil out of you and teach you the meaning of love, this you will pass on to your children, teach them how I loved you. She was busy loving other men to kill her child, those dark memories of her childhood defeated him. His grandfather didn't know it but when he touched her, he murdered her son.

Children who experience sexual trauma are closely associated with those diagnosed with posttraumatic stress disorder (PTSD). The psychological manifestations of this sort of abuse reveal itself as many types of emotional illnesses such as eating disorders, low self-esteem, anxiety, and even uncontrollable anger. These displaced emotions are often displayed in unhealthy relationships, and promiscuity, causing one to engage in high-risk sexual behaviors.

Da' Feat told me that he did what he did because he believes in demons; the church taught him about demons, he told me he didn't need a counselor, what he needed was an exorcist. The only way to quiet the demons was to give them what they desired, they craved attention, even negative would do. He said he would get a type of high from getting angry. In a fight, he would feel the rush of adrenaline so intensely that he would black out, all he would see is black, but he could feel his victim. Although blind with rage, he hardly ever missed his target. When he would get like this, he didn't feel the blows until after the battle was over, he loved that rush.

For Da' Feat, revenge was the sweetest joy! The only place for a madman like this was behind bars whether self-imposed or not, I do not know. No one ever loved him enough to figure him out, and he never stayed around long enough for them to begin to understand, they reinforced his doubt and pain. One woman even said to him, I know your mother and she is such a loving person, what happened to you? He said, "That's amazing, I'm just like her or rather, I'm just like the hands that made her." I'm giving you what she had to offer. Looking in from the outside, they saw how he had zeal for the saints of the church but demonized his own home.

The abused learn behaviors from the Abuser, he said he feared God and believed in Holiness; he told her that he had to learn the fear of the Lord and she had to learn to respect him, in his house you would live holy or get out! **The slave mentality...** He experienced this in his hometown of Jackson Mississippi, where his name was "boy" in the eyes of that racist society. He wanted to live as a respected man at home, even if it meant treating his family like servants who he would summon to bring him his food and favorite drink. Just as he had no identity in society, his children had no right to be themselves at home. Outside of his home, he couldn't look the white man in the eye for fear of disrespect, for he was only 3/5's of a man. Just as hatred was in his heart for those who treated him this way, he bred hatred in his home for his strict rules of Holiness. He had become that which he hated, the psychological chains of slavery had caused him to develop an attitude of his master which caused him to demand respect by force and fear, not by love.

    By no means did Da' Feat attempt to make the point that he was a victim, because through all his trials, he still retained the power to choose. He had a choice between right thinking and wrong, this he learned from his religious household, but no one taught him how to get through the pain. He couldn't even talk about pain, for pain was part of life. Pain doesn't end until life does, that's why heaven exists, and you can't expect earth to be like heaven, so he was taught. By now, you may be wondering what this young man did to end up in prison. Well, Da' Feat had robbed and raped multiple women in his short lifetime, and once he raped them, he murdered them. What he did to one of them in particular though, is what landed him in prison.

YOU TOUCHED ME, BUT HURT MY CHILD

He killed a woman, the woman he said he loved. How can a man kill the woman he loves? The two of them met at their crossroads in life, they both had made some wrong choices, and decided to pursue an education, they met on the campus of higher learning. Everyone knew they were meant to be, in fact, people thought they were already a couple although one did not know the other. Finally, after getting to know each other, the inevitable happened, and they fell in love. Da' Feat said it was the type of love that he had only felt for his mother and that's what caused him to do what he did. Destiny was a free spirited but strong-willed woman who refused to be controlled by a man, even by her own father.

Poor Da' Feat had his hands full. She was everything he ever wanted in a woman except for one thing, Destiny didn't understand his pain, she didn't know that Da' Feat loved her so much because finally a woman had replaced the first woman he had ever loved, his mother. He wanted Destiny all to himself. Although they would fight, the make-up was the best, she knew what to do, her name should have been pleasure for several reasons... Da' Feat said she was even built like his mother and come to think of it, they had the same walk. It was like once again; he felt the tender caress of momma for so many reasons when with his Destiny. This free and beautiful woman had one fault though; she did not want a quiet life, she was not a saint and Da' Feat wanted control, she was too free and powerful for him. Instead of loving her, he wanted to recreate her. Because of this, there was always friction and a lot of making love instead of allowing love to make them; it was the best, the way that the serpent moves is amazing, like lying with an angel until you get off the bed, he didn't understand her strength, she was rocking him to sleep.

He should have let her kill his demons, but because he couldn't control her, he bruised her. Remember his grandfather? Where did he get this from? If only Destiny could understand what prevented him from seeing her truth, she could have healed Da' Feat.

Destiny had her own past, she was looking for a man, not a son, and besides, she didn't know how to raise a boy, she only had "strong women in her family". One day, they got in a violent fight, and she told Da' Feat to leave. He left but came back because he had not taken all his bags and she opened the door for him to come back in and he raped and robbed her for everything she had, again and again until she was broken. Finally, Jericho had fallen! When Destiny allowed Da' Feat to destroy her, he saw his mother disappear and with her went all his pain! He finally realized his sin... All Da' Feat knew was how to break people for he was broken. When he left her, he left her for dead. She was no good to anyone else, finally he had marked her with his mark, every man after him would have to first destroy Da' Feat before he can see his Destiny. This was a strong woman, she loved him enough to heal him, what he took from her was only what she gave him... Life!

The prison of a man's mind...

Every man needs a Strong Woman... to unlock the prison cells of his mind. Such did Eve, to set Adam free, she gave him her fruit! Thank you, Destiny for yours, I love you Baby...

UNLEARN FEAR...

Right now, is the time for you to release the past! You've remembered it long enough. You've bought into the statement, "if you forget your past, you will do the same things that caused you to want to forget your past".

Those thoughts, the beliefs, superstitions, and fears of others are being torn down. The building of shadows has fallen, the Temple has been destroyed, that building where you once worshipped has been turned into rubble, it was built on fear, not knowledge. Knowledge of yourself is the greatest knowledge because there is where God lives. You find Christ in you, and in Christ Is God. For the longest, you have been told that you find Christ in a building called church. When you went there, did you find Christ? What did you hear them talking about? Life or death, faith, or fear? Our greatest fear is that we are powerful beyond belief, Nelson Mandela said that.

Parents want their children to remain home under their watchful eye for fear of their children's safety in the world. What happens when my child no longer needs me. Have you ever seen an eagle in real life?

UNLEARN FEAR

Perhaps you've seen a baby eagle in its nest imitating its parents by spreading its wings feeling the wind blowing between its feathers, although yet in the nest, they are getting ready for flight. Unfortunately, many of our parents were afraid of heights and they unknowingly raised us under the shadows of fear. Don't touch, don't handle, don't go there, don't talk to those people. Those people are drunks and tax collectors, they will cause you to fall, they will keep you from flying. Do you see those little eagles with their wings stretched wide, eager to soar and those who love them are saying no, if you get too high, you will fall and hurt yourself.

It is the heights that will enable you to catch the most wind...

What is being expressed to you are the limitations of our parents' inhibitions which have limited us. Protection doesn't come with keeping us from the enemy, protection is having knowledge of the enemy and its schemes, snares, and tactics. One day, you will meet what your parents have kept you away from and the enemy will tear you to pieces because the enemy knows all about you and you know nothing of him for your parents taught you to fear rather than rule.

To be exact, see this psychology; The highest Being is your spiritual self, and the ruler of your spiritual self is God. The first fear learned in the physical building is to Fear God and this taught to you by your parents. What child really loves the parent whom s/he fears? Fear in essence, is the lack of love. To fear God is to also neglect yourself for fear and love cannot exist together. Fear comes from the knowledge of what injures, those things that injure us we deny, we do not have a healthy relationship with those things which bring us pain. This is why the old things must pass away, this is why we must unlearn fear. For faith to make us free, we must destroy the old building, and with it, condemnation of ourselves and others.

Don't get so happy and think that you've made it because today you are on top in your career. Your marriage is going well, but don't get so happy. You are making all this money; money is the root of evil and God doesn't like ugly. As if you are ugly because you are making a decent living for yourself, and you have moved away from your small-town mentality. She thinks she's better than us because she has gone to college and now, he thinks he's somebody. Well, just like God can give,

He can take away, so we better not enjoy what God has Himself made possible. Don't even enjoy life because just as you come into this world naked, naked you shall return! She didn't pay for college anyway, it was that man who paid for it, if he leaves her, she'll fall back down on her face and who will she run to then?

This the mindset of those who fear God, the vengeful god of man. In fact, we must unlearn this god for he never was God, these are the teachings of man.

This is what fear looks like when fear has caused them to fall. They then teach us how to live in the same fear that has cut their wings. They are afraid to live so they talk about a heaven where God is, the same god, they taught us to fear. If your relationship is built on fear on earth, how will you get to heaven when you are afraid to Fly? This is why Jesus called Him Father, children seek to be like the father they love. Children who have been abused do what their father says, not for love, but for fear. In their hearts they curse the man who beats their mother and the hatred they see, they emulate for they have replaced love with fear and instead of casting fear away, they manifest it in their offspring. Unlearn this brokenness! First, we must ask, What is fear?

Fear is a perception; fear is a reaction to what is not understood. Since man is not infinite, and his understanding is limited, he learns fear. From your innate birthright, you are a master and ruler, you may not understand this, but didn't he call them gods? It is natural in this world but unnatural in the spiritual for you to make lord what you cannot rule. Simply stated, we were put here to rule and when we are unable to rule, we fear. Now comes worship, we cannot rule God so we must fear Him? Not at all, we must worship God by ruling Ourselves. We must master our reactions to the things of this world, we must rule every creature of the earth, by controlling our own minds. When we fail to master our thoughts, when our understanding is hindered, we create mythological figures, for deep within us, we know that we ourselves are gods.

When God places before us the opportunity for growth, He uses situations, conditions, beings, or things about which we do not understand, not for us to fear but for our growth. God instilled the fear of man into wild beasts, for man then to fear the beasts, the natural order of things has been perverted, fear is a perversion of the Truth. Truth is established by gaining knowledge, man has been put on the earth to learn and to grow. Many of you reading this book know this saying, "The fear of the Lord is the beginning of wisdom." But what does fear really mean, and whose fear is it anyway?

Do you remember that when you learned some of the most valuable life lessons, they came with pain or uneasiness? Well, this is one of those moments where you may get uneasy, so let's get ready for a mental shift. As understanding increases, fear dissipates, and God in Man is revealed.

The fear of the Lord does not mean what we have been made to understand. There is a natural gravitational force which draws all men to God through the knowledge of what has been created. When we gain knowledge of God's creation, we begin to understand the fear of the Lord. We must remove fear and replace it with joy as we come to understand what has come from Him, this is only the beginning of wisdom. With wisdom comes worship, we worship God in Holy reverence for what He has created, the knowledge of the Holy One is understanding. When man stops fearing God's creation and tearing it down to get to heaven, and starts mastering what is hidden in the earth, then is born God's

Son who does what his Father does and sees on earth only what his Father has shown him. Man alone, is the creator of fear. The object of fear is only An Image In the person's Own Mind, a reflection of *the mythological serpent religion of fear and death.*

Many are the malady brought about by fear. Malady is defined as a moral or mental disorder, a disordered state or condition. There is healthy fear and there is unhealthy fear. Unhealthy fear is closely related to false perceptions. The person who lives with unhealthy fear is diseased because that person is uneasy with life and waits for another world where he will one day live, allowing the life he has now to pass him by. Fear of the Lord is the beginning of wisdom. Wisdom is revealed when you realize that you've been blinded by fear, then you will turn and start Worshipping God with the life you live.

I was going to stop right there but you didn't understand what was just said, so let me clear it up. There is a god that they feared and then there is a Father who loves us...

Church Hurt, where does it come from?

REMOVING THE FIG LEAVES

I remember setting out for a 33-hour drive from San Antonio Texas to Tacoma WA. using only a paper map and a red 4-cylinder Hyundai Scoupe. Remember those paper maps? There was a time when the world was without GPS, and to get from point A to B, you had to plot and navigate your course of direction. It was just you, the road, and your intuition, using rest area maps as guidance along the way and the rest depended on your own innate abilities of navigating the terrains.

One of the most memorable sights during that drive was driving through the beautiful state of Oregon with its dense wilderness, hills, winding roads, and greenery. There seemed to be a constant fresh mist of moisture creating fertile soil and conditions for healthy tree and plant life. I can still remember the variety of colorful leaves on the trees unique to that part of the country. Reds, oranges, greens, reddish oranges which look like flaming fire, almost putting you in the mind of what the burning bush may have looked like. Bigleaf Maples, Douglas Firs, Red Cedars, and Ponderosa Pines, all covered with big vibrant and radiant leaves like outstretched hands collecting rainwater, mist, and sunlight for their food. For it is a mixture of sunlight, carbon and water which creates glucose as food for the different varieties of plant life in Oregon.

We could say in essence, it is this same mixture of sunlight, rain, and cool autumn nights, (yes, even darkness has its place) which creates for us the beautiful hues of the colors of life. It is not sunshine alone; darkness also creates life. There is a downside to this beauty though, the leaves that receive and process light for the trees, also prevent light from shining on the low lying, common folk of the ground, creating conditions of life for certain types of vegetation requiring only very little sunlight.

The key then is to dwell in a higher state of consciousness, where the light is.

How is it that the leaves *who* receive life can also hinder and conceal life? What do fig leaves have to do with the leaves of Oregon? A lot, when we consider that we are like those fig leaves that can receive light and at the same time, be a source of darkness, hindering light from others.

REMOVING THE FIG LEAVES

Covering with fig leaves is to block communication with the light, light cannot enter, and neither can light radiate if it is covered. This covering with leaves is indicative of man's contorted thoughts of himself. From one reason to another, man thinks less of himself because of what someone else has done to him or has spoken into him. What then are Fig Leaves? For those of you who have not seen or do not have knowledge of the significance of the Book of Genesis and haven't read that Adam covered himself with fig leaves to hide himself from God and his natural identity from the world after being touched by the psychological tongue of a serpent, the fig leaves represent a type of covering. Not just a form of clothing, but a mental garment which blocks the emission of the Son in man.

I stated in the beginning, that this book would not be theological, but just a quick reference to a spiritual teaching that many people may not be aware of, Jesus cursed a fig tree for not bearing fruit. There is no gain for you or the world in hiding your true nature because of someone else's objectivity of you. How long will you be who they say you are? People define you according to their own beliefs. Who Jesus is, well, let us understand what is meant by Jesus as the savior.

Jesus represents the true nature of all mankind, the Christ, the divine principle, and nature of Man. He cursed the unproductive fig tree, he cursed our unnatural nature, that nature that we ourselves have created to cover Hurt, pain, and indoctrination. The worst thing that could happen to us is that we would allow the vastness and availability of unlimited potentiality to have been summed up by a false perception created by what has happened to our physical selves, a physical act when I was 8 years old, when s/he did this or when they did that, to hurt me. It's time for us to destroy the entire Fig Tree, never will you bear fruit again! I will not share the fruit of your flesh with anyone else, I Am Great and wonderfully made, the true representation of the child of the Highest... Oh yes, that Divine Principle lives in me, It Is Me... When people ask you how you do all these great things, tell them because I Am. *(To Pharoah, Moses was God)*

This brings us to removing these fig leaves and the introduction of the meaning of the word subjectivity. Many of us have been made subjective to conditions and

situations of which we in that temporary moment and space had no control. Say this with me, "there was a time when to what I was subjected, I had no control, but now who I will become, better still, Who I Am, is up to me and only me for the I in me never changes.
Where are you, Adam?
I covered myself...

The first step in removing the leaves is to realize the power you have in your own transformation; especially since you were the one who covered yourself. Not the world in which we live but in response to the world in which we live, have we covered ourselves. It is not so much the act that hurts but your response, your own reactions which injure you. The minute you blame others, you render yourself powerless to change your environment. There is a reason that you were subjected. Are you ready for this? I really didn't want to get spiritual but what happened to the world is a spiritual problem. You were never subjected to anything, you were not really crucified, you were sacrificed to save some people who were placed on your journey; Christ is the living principle for all mankind. To have the appearance of being subjected, your true state must be higher than to what you have been subjected.

Your past was simply a State, to get to Tacoma from Texas, you must pass through Oregon. Texas was just a duty station while receiving training in the Army, today I live in another state, the State of Georgia. I really want a house on the beautiful Island of St. Thomas. Although physically in Georgia, I live in my mind in St. Thomas. With my mind, I see my Azimut Yacht parked in front of my house. With my mind, I am building a house in which I will live tomorrow.

We have the power to live in any state, be it one of restrictions, pain and hurt or in the state of "You are free to eat from any tree in the Garden" by the creative power of your own mind. You are not identified by any temporary state of subjection. Today you may be in the dry hot desert of Ft. Irwin California, building skills for desert warfare and tomorrow by the Power of Thought, Building Your House on an Island. Just because today, you are subjected to one state, the state of your tomorrow can change by how you see today. I just said to you that if you have been subjected to a state, the place from which you have originally come has to be

Higher. People and conditions have only been positioned in your life as your guides.

Sometimes the GPS comes in the form of bumps in the road; Your steps have been ordered. The hands that touched you are being used to exalt you; they too were subjected by circumstance. You met them in their sunken place, you now Live in a higher place, now you see the hands which have guided you, they weren't meant to destroy you, they caused you to pass through the fire to reveal you!

What is subjectivity? Subjectivity is defined as the quality, state, or nature of being by Merriam Webster's dictionary.

Your whole life, you've told God where you are without realizing the power of your own words which have alone positioned you. God doesn't tell us where we are, He creates everything that is possible and allows us to tell Him where we are. (Adam, where are you?) He lets us define our own states. Every person must live in their own conscious state of subjectivity and nowhere else. Don't allow those outside of you to affect the state in which you dwell, since God doesn't why should we allow those who do not value us to define us. If a person cannot define you, (no one can, except you) neither can anyone else determine your worth. The only power that anything on the outside of you has over you is the power of suggestion, even the Highest Power can only suggest to you who you are, you must subject yourself to the suggestion and become. In the case of the spiritual, to subject yourself to God, is to become more conscious of your spiritual man than you are of the physical.

Didn't I tell you that I would not make this book a spiritual one? Only to get to the root of pain do I use any particular religion or belief. The story of my pain began when I first heard that every man is a Sinner. The person teaching that doctrine of limitation, used the book of Genesis as the religion of death, so I must now use the same book to set the captives free.

Now that I have freed myself from the spiritual shackles of indoctrination and religious slavery, allow this book to offer a hand of inspiration to you. Let me clear the air, Adam was already great and walking in the Image of God when God created them. This is what happened, remember I told you that Christ is the Divine Principle of Man? Well, he was in the Garden! Hold on tight because I Am taking you into the Mental Garden of your mind, there are some creatures there that you alone are creator. Read that again, there are creatures in your garden that you placed there and are a source of your own torment and destruction! Notice that there were people and creatures present on the earth when Adam and Eve lived but were not identified as living. This was so because although we are interconnected, all that matters is what the individual believes exists in her/his world.

No matter how immense the universe, it will only be as vast or empty as your thoughts allow.

To get through this, we should consider a few words: Truth, Fact, and Scientific Fact. The Law of Life represents fact, then you have facts which can be proven Scientifically and finally, we have what is known as truth, the lesser of the three. Sounds strange? Let me explain. Have you ever heard someone argue a fact or disprove a fact? A fact is a thing which is known or has been proven to be true. The greatest fact is the principle upon which life is built. There is but one life, so there is but one principle and that principle is righteousness. Everything that contradicts righteousness has not life, it is a Lie. Truth is lesser because truth is relative to the individual. It's relative because man has the autonomy to decide what is true, but facts do not change. A man's truth can be a lie when it is placed side by side with facts.

The fact is that all creation is Life, and this life works in righteousness. Everything that is considered evil, man has created. The only creature on earth that has the power and ability to lie is man, for man has been given the power of life and death. If you don't understand thus far, please read this book again and consult your present state of consciousness to see who placed you in the very circumstance you are in right now. For the word **Consciousness** means realizing what your own mind has produced in your world. The bible teaches us that without faith, it is impossible to please God and then it gives us Abraham as an example of faith.

Why Abraham? I have been explaining to people for quite some time now who the serpent really is, but it is only since a few prominent people took on the topic that people are now listening. There is a You tube video titled, "They Were Not Deceived, They Desired Wisdom" which teaches that the reason Adam and Eve ate from the forbidden tree is that they were doing what God empowered them to do. God has placed in man a very powerful desire to learn and when man has mastered his environment, he creates new ones. God told the man to replenish the earth, so He gave them a desire to be productive. Faith comes when man has mastered his immediate plot of land, faith in the unknown keeps him from becoming stagnant or complacent, for his ultimate goal is to make straight the crooked path or bring righteousness to the earth. To do this, man must be a conqueror, first of himself then of the land.

What better example of this act than Abraham who left the known for the unknown. He left his father's house on a quest for Canaan. Adam and Eve did not eat because they were deceived, they ate because of a righteous void in man known as desire. To explain this, let's consider another story. In the desert from Egypt to Canaan, "from light to darkness", the people were bitten by venomous snakes and died. A cure for this venom was for Moses to build a bronze replica of a serpent and anyone bitten by a snake would be healed when he looks at the bronze snake. This bronze snake is known also as a caduceus, a symbol of health, healing, and medicine. Man is healed when he looks intently at himself for what ails him! There were deadly serpents living outside of the man but the deadliest of all serpents are those that are in man, they affect the life of the man.

If there is a serpent within, then all things will be seen from the serpent's perspective. It is said that the seed of the woman will crush the head of the serpent, the serpent lives in the head of man. Listen, the Seed of the Woman who is the Mother of all the Living, is the Christ nature or power of right thinking. To crush the head of the serpent, one must Think, change your thinking, leave one state, and fully enter another, then you will see the New Heaven and New Earth. Listen to this again, even while the Atom/Adam was in the Garden of paradise, he lived in hell, his body never left, there is but One World except for the world where the fallen man lives...

When the people left Egypt, they entered the wilderness of unfamiliarity. What is this but when we leave one state, and enter another not yet mastered by us, one of uncertainty; I don't have a job there, I don't know the highways and byways, I will get lost, I don't have any family there, I will be, <u>ALL</u> BY MYSELF. Again, I will Be All when I learn myself. *"The creation of Eve enabled Adam to identify with himself by seeing himself in the woman."* Leave your father's house Abraham and go to a land I will show you. It takes faith to do this. It takes boldness to face one's fears but to conquer fear, you must take it head on, for you must settle the matter in your mind before prosperity comes in the flesh. You must first see Canaan in your mind and live in Canaan before you get there, and your present condition will change, Faith is Substance, and it is Evidence. The desert represents the psychological state of destroying the old mental state and becoming a new you. When the old self dies, and the land is no longer familiar, it is then that you are fed from heaven. To remove the fig leaves, let us seek within to find the Christ.

When the Leaves Are Gone, I'm gone Shine...

I know a man who is the owner of a very successful housing developing company, we will call him Lernie. He was raised in a household where there existed the belief that man could only achieve so much before the sin of pride would rise up and cause a person to think too highly of themselves. His parents would say to him, "Don't count your chickens before they hatch" or "In this evil world, don't get so happy, happiness is here today and gone tomorrow." When you think you've made it God will "Knock you down", you can't get bigger than God! The one statement that really stuck with him throughout his life though was "God will knock you down!"

That statement seemed to really bother Lernie. He asked himself, why would God knock me down? Especially when there are so many bad things happening to people in this world and it seems like God doesn't stop tragic situations from happening, why would He knock someone down who believes in Him and are putting forth effort to do good, when so many are prosperous without considering good. Why knock me down for being proud of my accomplishments, isn't God the one who enabled it and made me possible. Doesn't prosperity come from applying principles of success which were established by God anyway.

As a small child, Lernie would hear his parents talking about people whose good fortune had run out, not by poor planning did they experience misfortune or setbacks but according to Lernie's parents, "God had knocked them down". Let me tell you a little about his folks. They were raising him and his 3 siblings in a modest home in Temple Texas. There they attended a small Bible believing Baptist Church where his parents were raised under the doctrine that "It is easier for a camel to pass through the eye of a needle, than for a rich man to enter into the kingdom of heaven" which it seems they believed literally. In their hearts, they believed that people who were wealthy did not and could not love and worship God since God did not enable one to gain riches, but the devil had more to give than does God. No, riches on earth did not come from God, every good thing from God is waiting on man in heaven. If a person strives for riches on earth, that person must deny God's order of things. Jesus didn't have a place to lay his head and why should man be better that God's only Son.

When Lernie's parents died, they did not own the house they were living in and neither had enough money in the bank or investments to pay for their own burials because of how they understood, "do not worry about what tomorrow will bring, tomorrow will take care of itself." Their children assumed the financial burden of paying for their funerals, they left their children with bills, not leverage. The two key lessons his parents instilled in him were the fear of God and the fear of hell. As a child, Lernie preached fire and brimstone to his peers, telling them that if they didn't go to church every Sunday, they were going to hell. After his parent's death, Lernie started to read the bible and one day he said he came across a passage found in the model prayer that Jesus taught in the book of Matthew, *"lead us not into temptation"*. He said this single passage in the bible caused him to shift his thinking. Why would Jesus have to ask God not to lead us into temptation.

All this time, Lernie had been going to church to serve a righteous God, why would a righteous God lead his children into temptation? This was the first time he had ever questioned the bible and sought answers outside of his parent's interpretation. He found that God doesn't tempt man, but certain desires come from within man and if man is the source of the evil desire, then man is also the source of the noble desire. One thought led to another, finally leading him to the book of Isaiah 65 where it says, *"They will build houses and dwell in them; they will plant vineyards and eat their fruit. No longer will they build houses and others live in them, or plant and others eat. For as the days of a tree, so will be the days of my people; my chosen ones will long enjoy the "Works of Their Hands,"* and before long, Lernie was on his journey because at that moment, he realized that he had a God given right to be successful and the only way to become successful was for his mind to master his hands. (*The mind is heaven and the hands the physical earth; on earth as it is in heaven*) He decided that his parents didn't build any houses, but he would, and just as someone built the house that his parents never owned, he would build houses that others would pay him for.

He understood this scripture well without the indoctrination of his parents. It is our God given right to honor God by "replenishing" the land, causing it to bring forth fruit. God is not jealous of us; He is proud of us as we lift our hands not only in church but also in business. Lernie helps us understand that wickedness is having the mind of God and not using it. Man can examine all the organs of the body including the brain but has been unsuccessful thus far in understanding what the Mind Is, it is heavenly, isn't Jesus from heaven? If you can't understand what I am saying to you, please stop going to church and do what Paul did; **Galatians 1:17**, *to find Christ, he stopped* "**going to church**".

The mind of man is just as vast and as difficult to understand as the mind of God. It is not wicked to live a successful life but, it is wicked to have an idle mind and do nothing with the power God has given us. This behavior has been learned by the parents and passed on to the children. We represent God not by being less, but we worship God by being His image on earth. A friend of mine invited me to a Friday morning Bible study at his home in an affluent neighborhood of John's Creek Ga. The first time I attended the Bible Study, he gave me directions and instructions on what to do when I get to his subdivision. I had to go to the security gate, tell the officer who I was there to visit, and the officer would call to notify the homeowner before allowing me to enter. Where he lives physically, expresses what he believes mentally.

He had to somewhere along his journey believe in his own abilities as a man. Not only is he a man but also, a man who serves God and has a nice place to lay his head. So, yes, we can love God and enjoy life at the same time. The excellence of man may be a shock to some because we don't all have the proper understanding of who man is and the reason for our existence. We were placed here on earth to be gods. You don't believe we were placed here to be gods? Read your Bible, up to this point, you haven't been reading it, you've been listening to someone else read it to you. When Moses saw God in the burning bush, *this is for those of you who **go to church**.* Remember when Moses asked to see God's face? God said, you can't see me and live; Moses saw God's face in the burning bush and God said Moses, you will be god to Pharoah. Listen church folk, THE FACE OF GOD IS MAN! We are the invisible Mind of God revealed...

This is the Love of God revealed in man; that man should reveal the invisible God by cultivating the earth. Not by shrinking but by being grand, just as a millionaire would not subject her/himself to a homeless shelter, the children of the King should not live like powerless peasants. Our creations on earth reveal what we believe. Don't hide your excellent identity, fearing that your life will not be pleasing to God if you get too high. God is exalted and wants us to be where He is, so, let us remove every leaf that keeps us from being...

Whatever it is you want to; **Be!**

A TRUE LOVE STORY

What do we suggest to our children when we say to them, "you can't." What about when we say to them, God said, Nothing good lives in you... You are a sinner good for nothing and born for death. Suggestion is the key to faith, belief, and hope, but it could also cause you to fall. I want you to think about something, I really need you to consider this and decide what happened, what was the cause of this woman's troubles.

Her name is, I won't call her name, but her initials are SAF, in fact, I will call her Saff. Second thought, I'll tell you her name, you probably already know exactly who I'm writing about, or you know someone like her. Her name is Safronica, a complicated name but a very simple person. She is a very spiritual person because of her upbringing, her family believed in spirits and the power of incantations and believed that words have power. One day a priest prophesied to her that she would experience troubles on her path to happiness. He said, although she had been through failed relationships, love was coming, she would meet a man who would be different from the others. It may seem like it's difficult at first but stay with it because a life of happiness is going to come out of it all, this man will be the one for you.

Seems cut and dry, doesn't it? Decide for yourself if the things that followed happened because of what the priest suggested or because of what she believed. Remember, we are all priests, we all possess the ability to speak what is or what is not. We all have the power to call a person by a name, for evil or for good. We give people power to be who they are in our lives. We can write a person in our lives or out, just as Jesus identified his disciples by name, we can write people out of our lives. They will become as significant or insignificant as we allow them to. It is we who identify them as fisherman or saint...

Saff was married for several years, maybe 11 or 12, and has 2 beautiful daughters who have grown up into powerful and successful women, neither are married but are independent of men, making a living for themselves and a good one at that. In fact, I remember a conversation where the oldest asked after her mother and father divorced, "Mom, don't you get tired of waiting on a man to make you happy?" Saff replied, "God put us here, not to be alone, but to love and be loved, if it weren't for your father and I, you wouldn't exist, you'll understand one day, you are not even complete without a man." Her daughter has always remembered that statement to this very day, that was 10 years ago, Saff is now 56 years old. She met a man online one day through a friend of a friend who needed a friend who had money, long money, so Jay set it up. He was a doctor, practicing medicine in Portugal and looking for a nice woman to settle down with, someone to share his life with. When he met Saff, she fit the description, not only was she doing well in life, but she was also beautiful. She looked like she belonged on a Caribbean postcard, with her clear light bronze complexion, and flowing hair, I believe she was from India or close to it.

Let me tell you about Saff's life, marriage, challenges, and hardships and how she was rescued by this handsome Dr. who became the man of her dreams.

The story begins with Saff's close friend with whom she had been friends since childhood, her name is Jay. The two were inseparable, they would wear the other's clothes, keep the other's children and even dated two brothers at the same time, they were like sisters, they were so close. They even got in trouble together;

once, Jay helped Saff jump on Saff's boyfriend Rick when they caught him kissing a woman around the corner from where Saff and Rick lived. It happened one day as Jay and Saff were on the way to Saff's house, they saw two people standing on the front porch kissing. Jay said, "Saff, isn't that Rick's 10 speed bike parked in that yard?" Saff said, "yes, as she noticed two silhouettes holding each other closely as it rained lightly. Well, they drove one block over and waited for Rick to come riding by and knocked him off his bike with the car door and told him, "That's what happens to pigs when they play in mud!"

    Now Rick was a 29-year-old man using a 10-speed bike for transportation because he thought he did his best driving after a bottle of cheap brandy or was it a bottle of Thunderbird the cops found in his car when they arrested him for his 3rd DUI? Whatever it was, it was something inexpensive, because he lived with Saff and worked at the temp agency, not earning much money. He always had a clean pair of Nike's on but wasn't even on the lease with Saff. Come to think of it, Rick was the type who would borrow Saff's car while she was at work and then pick her up late with the car smelling like melted wax and cheap perfume. Saff would often find aluminum foil tucked down between the console and the seat, but she didn't know why.

Despite his habits, she loved him, she believed that a woman should never be alone, everybody needs somebody, even if that somebody makes mistakes. Sometimes we learn to function better in disfunction, especially when we believe we don't deserve better. What is it that causes some people to expect more and others to expect less? Is this behavior learned from childhood? Saff's relationship with Rick, was not all bad, they had their share of high moments as well as their lows. Don't we all experience growth pains when learning to live with someone? Well, hard times sometimes build bonds, or at least causes us to normalize dysfunctional behaviors long enough until we learn to thrive in toxicity as did Saff.

She agreed to marry rick since they had built a bond, she knew him, and he knew her. Although their marriage lasted for 12 years, there were many restless and sleepless nights of Saff wondering when would Rick get home, and if he would be back in time to take her to work the next morning. There was good that came from their marriage though, they had two daughters together before they finally divorced, whom she loved and cherished dearly.

Saff had to come to the realization and face what she feared for a long time, Rick had a drug and alcohol problem. She tried to ignore it, but his habits grew worse over the years and could no longer be covered up. Since Saff had to function as the bread winner, she was always looking for ways to increase financial security for the family and one day she landed a job with the Atlanta School Systems, where she has been employed for close to 20 years now. She never really got over Rick, he was all she knew, and she was hurt by the divorce and said to herself, "All I want is to be happy, why is it so hard to find someone for me?" After Rick, Saff engaged in several different relationships over a length of time, none of which lasted more than 2 or 3 years, and it seemed as if she would live her life alone.

She had accomplished a lot without the deadweight of Rick, she purchased a nice house which will be paid off in less than two years and she has a sizeable pension coming from the School System when she decides to retire. From the outside looking in, one may say that Saff has made it, but she still desires the company and attention of a man, someone to share her life with. Isn't that what we all want from life, just a little piece of happiness? Well, one day Saff's dreams of happiness and love came true.

During a special program at church, a guest speaker spoke to Saff about her life. How could he know these things about my life, did someone tell him these things about me, am I being set up? Everything he said about me, he couldn't possibly know without someone close to me telling him. God is this what I've been waiting on? Has my ship finally come? I'm a good person, I'm pretty, I don't stay out all hours of the night, I have my own money, I know how to be a good friend, why wouldn't a man want me? I at least want to get in the car and see my man in the driver's seat going with me to the store. I want someone who I can wake up with early on Saturday mornings and go to the coffee shop, sit outside in the cool morning breeze and sip coffee, someone for me. I want my man to come up behind me while I'm cooking, embrace me in his strong arms and whisper sweet things to me, is that too much to ask?

Saff jumped for joy at the news of good fortune predicted by the priest. Praise God, love is coming she exclaimed as she put a crisp $188.00 in the offering. This was not payment for the word, this was just her doing her part to support the ministry which supported her spiritual growth.

Saff left that service convinced that she would soon meet Mr. Right. Is it possible to truly meet Mr. or Mrs. Right? Or do we create them in our own minds? Do they exist or do we get from life exactly what we see into it? Is Mr. or Mrs. Right born or are they made and formed in our own minds? We need a Mr. or Mrs. Right to be for us what we are missing but does such a person exist, are they being themselves or simply who you need them to be, the person you see?

Her friends arranged the meeting between Saff and Charles, Prince Charles because he was everything, she wanted him to be. She first saw a picture of him and was well pleased. He was about 6' 1" and a carved 198lbs with light skinned smooth complexion, born in Portugal, his father Portuguese, and his mother Guyanese, handsome wasn't the word, Saff thought to herself, "this can't be true," "Oh my god!" Charles was a physician in

Portugal, following in his mother and father's footsteps who created a good life for him. He would come to the states from time to time, he loved Miami Florida, it reminded him of home but away from home. When he laid eyes on Saff, she was everything he had hoped she would be, he could see it in her from the start.

Charles and Saff would talk on the phone for hours, laughing and finding so many commonalities shared between them, it was like a dream, yes, they do come true... It was on one of his trips to Miami that the two met for the first time. They began their day together enjoying freshly grilled fish, from an oceanside open patio restaurant. To really set the mood, the sounds of Caribbean music played softly in the background. Saff said ever since that day, she hears the melodic sounds of steelpans playing softly whenever she thinks of Charles.

Once finished eating, he pulled her chair out from the table and assisted her to her feet, the perfect gentleman, his father would do the same for his mother. They ordered a drink with a little umbrella coming out of a pineapple to go and sipped on it as they strolled through a shopping mall. S.A.F (*you'll understand the initials at the end*) wearing open toe sandals with an ankle bracelet made in India, her free-flowing skirt, made of white linen blowing in the wind, it was a picture of paradise. Charles, wearing a white short set and brown sandals on his feet, on his wrist, an 18k gold bracelet, glistening in the sun, this was the moment SAF longed for, she wanted this dream to last forever. As the day came to an end, they returned to their hotel where they lounged near the bar well into the night getting familiar. Their trip lasted for the weekend and SAF had to return home, but she carried Miami with her in her mind. As the months went by, SAF and Charles grew closer and closer, he told his parents about his new woman and SAF told her children, she was so happy, and her daughters were happy for her too. They couldn't wait to see the man who had brought sunshine back into their mother's life.

    Not long after the Miami trip, Charles sent SAF a gift. Since she admired his 18k yellow gold bracelet, Charles decided to send her jewelry of her own. He sent her 2 beautiful herringbone necklaces, a toe ring, and two tennis bracelets to prove his devotion and appreciation for her. He told her that he wanted to spend the rest of his life with her. SAF couldn't wait to wear some of her gifts to work, to share her happiness with her co-workers who doubted that she had found a real-life prince. People act as if they are happy for you until they see your good fortune, and then it seems as if their joy turns to jealousy, why is that? Well, many of her co-workers who doubted that she had met a doctor but told her how happy they were for her, now started to talk about her saying, things like, "she better be careful, he probably has 3 or 4 women in his country. With all the women in Portugal, why would a Dr. need to come to America to get a woman?"

Before SAF's story became a reality, her co-workers seemed so happy for her, now that her dreams had become a reality, where did the jealousy come from? Those who seemed happy for her in the beginning, seem now to be against her, maybe it was the jewelry she never wore. Or maybe they could relate with her more when she was lonely, maybe her previous state of loneliness was all so familiar to those who were also miserable. Well, despite what they said, SAF's happiness continued and their feelings for one another grew stronger and stronger as time went on.

A TRUE LOVE STORY

Charles decided to bring his medical practice to America, he and his partners wanted to build a Dr's office in beautiful San Diego California. He told SAF that he wanted her to sell her house and marry him. Saff could not believe this was happening, it was too good to be true. When God blesses you, sometimes, it feels unbelievable even if it's exactly what you've asked Him for. When thoughts become things, sometimes we forget that the things were first our thoughts. When our thoughts become the experience, we either thank God or blame the devil... Such is our Nature. Well, Charles wanted to show her that his love for her was true by sending her another gift. This time, a monetary gift, Charles sent her $25,000, but because of the amount of money being sent at one time, this caught the attention of U.S Customs and the money was seized.

Charles contacted Saff who helped sort out the matter and to answer the reason for such a large transfer. Well, after having to pay nearly $2,500 to customs, a trip out of town and over 10 legal documents later, the matter was resolved, and her money was freed. He did this to help her pay off her mortgage since he didn't want her to sell during the current market, they talked about how the housing market was changing, and decided that then wasn't the time to sell. Wait awhile said Charles, and the house will be worth much more, a brilliant businessman was Charles.

Now Saff had established a wonderful pension over the many years she worked for the school system, she would use that for retirement, so she thought. Never did she dream that she would meet someone like Charles who could support her for the rest of her life. Well Charles needed her just as she wanted him. To begin work on the Dr's office complex, Charles needed a citizen of the U.S. to represent him, and since his soon to be wife would manage a part of the operation, Charles needed SAF to also invest. Some business associates met with Saff to discuss the plans and the requirements of owning a business in America by a foreigner and helped her understand her role as his soon to be wife and business partner.

Her monetary investment was pivotal in the success of the business. The groundbreaking event would be scheduled 6 months from the date of their visit to allow processing time. Not only would Saff be a wife but a partner and manager. A meeting and date were again set for her to see Charles, this time in San Diego, Charles was flying in with his parents to celebrate the business and to meet his future. When Saff arrived in San Diego, she was met with unfortunate news, Charles' parents telephoned Saff to tell her that Charles had been detained by customs for bringing in too much undeclared cash, about $300,000.

It was first said that he would be released after 36 hours, but 36 hours turned into 90 days and 90 days turned into Saff having to return home without seeing Charles or meeting his parents. Charles was finally able to call Saff after the initial 36 hours to explain what happened and how the groundbreaking plans for the medical complex would continue. Saff and the business associates would take the lead in Charles' name. Since his money had been seized by customs, he needed Saff to use her retirement to go forward with the plans. To get things started, only $40,000 was needed from Saff which Charles agreed to repay her, and the partners would add the rest of the $120,000 needed for licenses, permits, inspections, plans, deposits, and payments.

This was really happening, and Saff was amazed by her new life, the life of which she had only dreamed.

During the 90 days of Charles' detainment, he called Saff and told her that there were some immigrants who had also been detained and he is serving as a physician for them, performing minor surgeries and treatments in the daily infirmary. What God has for you is for you, said Saff, "even when the devil tries to stop your plans, God confirms and expands your purpose." After the 90 days of detainment were over, Charles returned to Portugal and sent for Saff since they would marry soon and he wanted her to meet his parents, and by coming to Portugal, not only would she meet them but also his friends and other family members.

    Things were set for Saff to purchase the airline ticket with the money that Charles had wired her when at the last minute, Charles called Saff and broke the terrible news to her, he had been betrayed by his business partners in California, they never purchased the land, and they had fled the country with the money. The attorneys who pretended to close the deal were fake, the whole thing was staged from day one, Charles is now facing legal trouble and Saff has lost $40,000 of her retirement money. Now over the next few days, Saff could not get in contact with Charles, all she could do was imagine what he may now be facing with the authorities because of others who had invested in the venture. Finally, Saff received a call from Charles and was so happy to hear that he was at least safe but wondered what they would now do.

Well said Charles, I love you and we are going forward with our plans. Send me back the money that I sent you for your ticket to Portugal, and I am coming to the states to marry you. He said, "If all else goes wrong, I want to share my life with you, and besides, I'm a Dr. and a very good one, I'll make the money back, but I don't want to be without you any longer." Well, Saff sent the money back and to this day has not seen Charles in person. Saff spent money two more times on a plane ticket to meet "Prince Charles", in Georgia and in Florida and each time, he gave her an elaborately fabricated story of why the meeting did not take place. Not only were Charles' stories fabricated, but Charles himself was a creation of Saff's own mind... She had never physically laid eyes on him, she had only spoken to him on the phone and online, and yet she believed all his silly concocted stories.

That wonderfully romantic trip to Miami never happened, it was what SAF hoped their meeting would be like, she allowed herself to be deceived because of what she hoped for. Remember the Garden of Eden story about Eve, it was not what the serpent fed Eve, it was what Eve wanted to eat that defiled her. Just as SAF created a fantasy to live in, to some extent, we all do the same with our own minds. People reveal to us who they are and because we need them to be who we need them to be, we do not allow them to be themselves, so then, they deceive us of everything we have and leave us empty. We create our own Serpents... I shared this story with you because the title of this book is Church Hurt and I want to teach you the true meaning of the story of Adam and Eve. We are Adam and Eve, and we continue to create our own devils.

And now the Conclusion...

Safronica was abused by this experience, the man who finds her next will have to lie down with demons from her past, but don't be so quick to criticize her. How many of you have had to sleep with demons before you finally penetrated the person you were lying down with? Do you know how many demons you've encountered before finally meeting the person beneath the hurt? "My name is Legion," he answered Him, "because we are many." Why do you think that oft times when you meet a certain type of woman, she gives you a false name? You may think it's a joke, but she is telling you the truth, so trust her, you are meeting her altered ego, the person she became in response to failed relationships with broken men. *We become who we must become to keep living...* Some of you have become someone totally different because of your encounters with demons, not demons but People! Hurting people... You had to become someone else to love the person that you are with. As a result, do you even know who you are? So don't be critical of Safronica until you think about your own created circumstances.

    Your family doesn't even recognize you anymore because you want to love the person that you are with. Don't you think for a second that the person you are with is the person who loves you until you deal with their demons. You must first love her demons to love her. So, brother, that woman could never love you until you deal with someone else. Although her body is there, her mind is somewhere else, if you pay close attention, you will hear her talking to you, talking to him. It's because she is thinking about him! She could never let you into his space, the place where only his hat belongs. You've showered her with so many material gifts, but she's still carrying his last name. No, it's not on any documents, forms or legal paperwork, his name is written on her heart. Why do you think she can't have certain conversations without shedding tears? So, no my brother, the person you're loving, is not the person you can see. Until that woman has healed, she has you lying down with the Mrs. she used to be when she was with Charles... *Remember Saff's friend Jay?*

Ladies, watch him, look very closely, look at what he's showering you with, he's trying to make up to her, those gifts with your name on them may really be for her, he's dealing with demons too...

They told him that Lazarus was dead and by now, Lazarus was smelling, but you know he is not dead, he just smells like that because of Hurt. Regardless of what the world says, your child is not dead. Go back and get your child. You know exactly where you left her, I can hear your child crying and I know exactly who I'm speaking to, I see you Safronica...

WHY DO YOU LOOK LIKE THAT?

We've been doing the same things the same way for so long that, little by little, we are forgetting how to think for ourselves. You may not agree with that statement, but agree or not, your success reflects how you've been thinking. Those who consistently think differently from the masses are the ones who are usually rulers of the masses...

Why do you remove the leg off the Thanksgiving Turkey? The way you make that turkey taste on Thanksgiving Day, it seems like you invented basting and roasting turkeys. No, my mother makes it better than I do. I've been using her recipe for years; you haven't tasted a good bird until you taste my mother's turkey. I'm just wondering though, why do you remove the leg off the turkey before you cook it? My mother removes the leg from hers, that's part of the recipe; that's the trick, that's why you are smacking your lips and dripping juice all over the place because the leg is missing...

Well, the recipe continued for 100 more years until they all got to heaven, where they were having

Thanksgiving one Sunday... in heaven. The daughter looked at her mother and said, mother there's something I've always wanted to ask you, why do you remove the leg from the turkey? Her mother said, "it's my mother's recipe, don't ask why." Well, the daughter wasn't satisfied with that answer, so she went and asked her grandmother who was now making some delicious brown gravy and basting the turkey in all its juices. The granddaughter asked her grandmother, grandmother why did mother remove the leg from the turkey, she said it was your recipe. Grandmother looked at her and said, I don't know why your mother removed the leg from her turkey but the reason I did it was because my pan was so little...

Keep on having church like you've been having church and living life like you've been living life and treating people like you've been treating people, and you will continue to get what you've always gotten. Church changes when you take a step back, walk out of the building and look at the church. Life changes when you take a step back and reframe your thinking. People will also change when you take a step back and look at what makes people appear to be who they are and you will find out that all these relationships, experiences and interactions first take place in you.

Before you go to church, you form the experience. Before you start living your life, you judge your parent's lives. Before you get into relationships with people, you name them even before you know them. The world you experience is the world you've shaped and formed, and now that you know that people are living with cracked, dented, and small pans, I ask you, **Why Do You Look Like That?** No, not your physical appearance but how you see. So many of our neighbors are living with torments from their past but are attempting to live and enjoy life as best as possible without exposing their past. What happens when you encounter one who is possessed with so-called demons who make them scream out loud or even curse with every conversation or maybe every word in the conversation is profanity.

Are you well enough to help heal? Or will you turn your back on those who are calling out for your help because something is just wrong with them...

So many of us are living with suppressed hurt and pain that disfunction has been normalized. A new culture of low morals has concealed the culture of morality and sound judgement, causing us to use words such as ratchet to accentuate unbecoming characters and personalities, calling good bad and downright nasty attitudes boujee, rich in material, but poor socially. When chains are placed on the mind, it takes a free mind to see the chains. Those bound, adapt to a lifestyle of limits, creating a philosophy and even a religion which justifies limited mindsets. After living for an extended time in chains, we suppress thoughts of freedom, in fact freedom becomes bondage. We consciously forget who we are and after suppressing thoughts for so long, we cause areas of the brain to decrease in its functioning until finally, we enter a demented state where we no longer recognize members of the group as their original selves but only as shadows of who they used to be.

The darkness of her womb...

A lady with early-stage dementia shared her story of abuse with me. She told me of her childhood trauma, it's strange that some memories were distant and distorted, but not the traumatic experience, it was fresh in her mind like yesterday. It happened when she was

WHY DO YOU LOOK LIKE THAT

just a little girl, about 9 or 10, her mother and father were no longer together, and her mother had remarried.

She said she remembered being awakened in the middle of the night by a hand under the covers of her bed. At first, she said she thought it was her mother tucking her in at night, so she paid it no mind. As time went on, she realized that where she was being touched, her mother wouldn't touch her there, she started to wake up to see exactly what was going on and who owned the hands that prey. With one eye opened, she couldn't see his face, only his arm because he would crouch on the floor like a beast so as not to be seen. This continued for a while until the little girl understood what was really happening and *"woke up",* taking hold of the hand touching her and instantly a face appeared. The man was the source of the pain in her womb!

Well, she came up with a plan, she told her mother, but her mother didn't believe her, so she took matters into her own hands, she was a smart little girl. Since the bed was positioned against the wall and her sister, her stepdad's biological daughter also slept in the bed, she would trade places with her, she would become her sister and her sister would take her position. The wall was her defense, he would have to reach over his own daughter to get to her from the other side. After years had gone by and this little girl had prayed the unanswered prayer for her stepdad's death, she learned to live in his world, she became who she needed to become so that she could keep living. By the age of 17, she was strong enough to save herself since she realized that no one else would...

    She saved up the money he would give her from time to time and purchased a bus ticket to go live with her father's sister in another state. As I continued to listen, a strange feeling started to come over me, it started to feel as if I could relate to the world in which she lived, one where to win, you must play by the other person's rules. In an unexpected way, her story started to shift, and it started to feel as if deep inside of her, she in some way took advantage of the abusive relationship and manipulated the man.

    She said but I have to level with you about something and her story began to change. She started to describe her stepfather in a way that I did not expect, she said, "He was a big burly man and a protector." Someone who ran his household according to his rules, what he said was the law and no outsiders came between him and his family. She continued saying that they always had good food to eat, and everything else they needed. Then she started to describe his physical appearance, and it really began to puzzle me.

He had large strong hands, hands that looked like they could crush a bowling ball with one squeeze, and everyone was subject to these hands. Although strong, he was gentle to those he loved, when he embraced you, you could feel his protection. Those he considered as loyal, lived close to him, but those he couldn't trust, lived on the outside. As his favorite, she would get almost anything she wanted, she felt like the lady of the house, it was like she forgot about herself and wanted to please him. Being accepted by him made her feel special, all she wanted was to belong. To be accepted by a man with so much power gave her worth, no matter the abuse, she learned to appear to live with it for her own benefit.

It was almost like the privilege outweighed the abuse, she said she felt special because he said she was. She ended the story by telling me that her sister ended up in a mental hospital in chains. No, not physical chains but psychological. When she left, her stepdad turned to his own daughter who after years of abuse became pregnant with two of his children. Her sister had been telling her mother of the abuse but was constantly scolded as a liar by her mother who said she was a mischievous child having sex with the neighbor's son. By the time of the second child, the emotional distress caused her to have a psychological breakdown, which in turn, led to her mother, the one who gave birth to her, gladly admitting her to a mental institution. To cope with the abuse, that little girl had to lose her mind.

How often do we lose our minds and not even realize that we have had to become someone else to live in his world?

Before I bring this book to a close, let me share a story with you from the Bible concerning chains of bondage and becoming someone else. There was a man from the lost tribe of Dan who lived in the tombs. No one was able to restrain him, even with chains. He often had been bound with shackles and chains but had snapped off the chains and smashed the shackles. No one was strong enough to subdue him. And always, night and day, he was crying out among the tombs and in the mountains and cutting himself with stones. At one time, this man was just as normal as you and I are, but his life experiences caused him to appear as a wild man. His demons were many, for he had lived in a world filled with demons, what do you mean demons? Well, they were everyday people getting along by any means necessary, even if it meant trampling down others. People are not demons, it's just the way we must act sometimes... The story goes on to say that Jesus cast those demons out of the man, and he came to himself and started to live again. The main point of that story is that the tribe of Dan was one of the original tribes but were somehow lost.

We are all like this man in chains, a tribe lost, living in the hills of bondage and chains, who will come for us? The people who caused our pains are they who have labeled us as lunatics and possessed and have bound us in chains to be forgotten. Isn't that how it is?

You've had to become someone different with every relationship and almost every interaction so that people who were not secure in who they are could feel good about themselves, as you fade away. For Bob, you had to become Sheila: For Julia, you had to be Steve; for

Kim you had to become Paul and by the time you're finished being who everyone else needed you to be, you become unrecognizable even to yourself. In this unrecognizable state, they cast you off to the hills, they have no more use for you. You have become like Adam, even God is looking for the real you; Adam where are you? These are the demons I speak of, the labels, the hands that have touched us,

The Hands That Prey...

Some of us are afraid of our Serpent, some of us understand that the Serpent must be exactly what it should be so that Man may be exactly who God says they are. The key to success in this world is for you to remember...

Reach back in your subconscious and remember who you are, who you were before man put his hands on you and gave you an identity; you must be ruler of the serpent.

Many of you don't believe that you have become someone else so I will end this book so that you can get back to who they need you to be so they can keep on having Church.

Religion is regarded by the common people as true, by the wise as false, and by the rulers as useful.
Lucius A. Seneca

THE END.

It doesn't matter if I've had to trudge a mountain of despair in my lifetime, only to find one stone of hope for the group, isn't that what makes life worth living? Well then, there is no better place for us to end this book than with a discussion about the stone of hope.

There is a man who loved his daughter dearly, just as daughters are to their fathers and sons are to their mothers, the two were inseparable, she was truly a father's girl. If dad was cutting the grass, she would be riding on the back of the lawnmower. Anytime dad started the car, no matter what the destination, daughter was in the back seat with her teddy bear and little fuzzy puppy, they all were a team.

As she grew, there were father daughter dances, professional days at school, and dad would be her presentation. Learning to drive, dad was the instructor. Mom was there but the young lady was truly a father's girl. The day before she would take the written test for her permit, she was so happy to finally be able to drive a car with dad in the passenger seat. Sadly, one day while at a friend's house and as they were standing on the edge of the sidewalk, a drunk driver ran up on the sidewalk, and mowed her down. When her dad received the news, he was devastated, he thought he would just lie down and die with her. He was only minutes away from the friend's house to pick her up, she was standing outside waiting on him. This man said in a statement to the news channel, "My daughter has been taken away from me, I will never again be the person I was with her!" "Who I was with her has laid down on the ground and died never to live again!"

His statement rings so true, who we are with one person, the way in which we know and are known in one relationship can never be the same in another. The dad his daughter knew was not known by even his own mother, for she was not his precious daughter. Although raised by his mother, she was unable to experience the relationship of father and daughter and neither could his wife, although intimate like no other, she could not be daughter. So, I ask this question to you, who are you? Do you know yourself or do others reveal you? You may be quick to answer that question by saying you know who you are and who others believe you are doesn't matter. So, I ask you again, who are you?

Have you ever had to decide which one of your children would eat before you lie down for bed at night because there was barely any food in the house? Even worse than that, have you ever had to decide which one of your children would be executed by the mafia for an unpaid gambling debt? What if after you made that decision, the one you decided to save was the very one the mafia decided to kill. How would you live with the child who felt like you wanted him to die? Do you know who you would be after a situation like that? The person you were before that incident, would possibly never live again. Situations and circumstances have made us and who we are, is not known until life has made its impression upon us. You are a complex being, who you are must become known by the people you live with and the experiences you have on earth.

We are such gregarious beings that we are unknown if there were not people to describe us. There is no wonder that we cannot see our own faces without only seeing a reflection. It is not we who can see ourselves, but others must tell us how we look and without them, we only see reflections. This is why it is said, "I'm ok when the group is ok and if the group is not ok, I'm not ok."

Everything about human life and existence is centered on relationships. Relationships first with our parents, then with siblings, then with other children and finally with other adults and let's just say other adult things we experience in life. Did you notice that in identifying relationships, we have not mentioned relationships with ourselves. It may be safe to say that who we are depends on who we have been next to. You may have heard or have said to someone yourself, "I don't need you! Go, I don't ever want to see you again!" If you've been in any sort of intimate or emotional relationship with the person you are sending away, did you know that a part of you has also left, to never live again. The words of a marriage vow rings louder and clearer, the words, 'until death do us part', which should read, until death does its part. Why? Because, when the two are divided after having been one, the one (the entity created by the joining of the two, the spiritual being) dies when they become two again.

Jesus and the Father are one, who they are together, could never be the same apart. Have you realized that we are like God in that God is only known through relationship? It has taken the entire world a lifetime to begin to know God, and it takes a lifetime for us to know who we truly are. The relationship dies during the divorce.

Do you agree with that? Agree or disagree, the power of relationships is present even in the animal and plant kingdom or the Eco-System. An ecosystem is a complex system of living organisms, their physical environment, and the interrelationships between them within a given area. In other words, eco systems are the environments that thrive best when able to properly react to a state of constant change, heat, cold, moisture, dryness, light, darkness, etc. There exists another invisible component of a healthy ecosystem, the proper amount of pressure.

Without pressure or the presence of an invisible and spiritual force, the system falls apart. These forces don't come as you may expect from outside of the system but are created by the system. Although the force exists on the outside of the system, there is a certain portion on which the individual community takes for itself to live. The size of the force decides the life of the

THE END

system. There are natural stresses and pressures within the environment which are acting on the environment to cause one environment to differ from another. When substance is taken from one environment and placed into another without having come to life in response to the stresses, and pressures of the new environment, either the life that is introduced dies or it affects the new environment causing it to expand or collapse.

Plants and animals thrive in their environments and there is no wonder that when transplanted into another, the ecosystem is sometimes adversely affected. Therefore, it should not be a wonder that certain animals cannot thrive together and maintain a healthy environment.

One may say that constant change, pressures, and stresses of life create the lords of life. Keep reading, and you will begin to see the image, the substance of the flame, the Stone of Hope. Because you have done this, because you have created this environment, by the sweat of your brow will you eat your food. God placed us here to think, the sweat of the brow means that to eat and to live, we must think. In essence, we will only eat what we are able to see and to think about. Because of our relationships, some of us have an appetite for the least of all meats; spam and others for steak and still, others for the freshest and crispest chards. Your hands can only prepare what your mind has brought to the table.

Just to clear the air, God does not curse those He loves.

When telling Adam, "By the sweat of your brow will you eat your food", Adam was blessed by those words and not cursed, the enemy has Convoluted God's Word. God was seen as living in the sky by ancient minds, where the sun and the moon lives. From the sky comes rain onto the earth, when man works, he sweats. When God works, he sweats and His sweat drips to the earth and vegetation grows. (They didn't understand the purpose of rain) Because of our relationships with premature and superstitious minds, we see the curse rather than the blessing. By causing man to think for his food, man has created everything that exists in his world, and it comes from heaven, the sky where God lives; sky=head, the hidden thoughts of the man.

Out of darkness have I called my son. Every object, every person, every entity that is present on Earth

THE END

has an image that was first invisible, seen by God only. Although you were unseen, God called your name.

When we can come face to face with the physical things on Earth and think properly and see as God sees, then we will be the image of God, seeing in this world, what God sees, being in this world who God sees and having in this world what God has laid up for His children to have. We are presented with all things unimaginable so that who we may become also cannot be imagined. I say unto you, no matter what you have been through, those things have only come that the Son, Sun might shine! Learn to think properly about every experience and you will see God in all. *The Church is a living breathing organism, and the world is Mental...*

AMEN... Ra!

Don't get upset about my ending this book with Amen Ra. You've been saying it at the end of your prayers all your life whenever you've uttered amen. Now, read about what it means in the author's number 1 book: ADAM Man Convoluted, but God.

Man must first know himself and all things will become visible, even the enemy of man

About the author:

Thomas L. Hampton II, born April 21, 1971 in the Divine Savior Hospital, York S.C. His parents were Virginia and Thomas Hampton founder of "The Chosen Few Ministry". On January 10, 2006, he was spiritually awakened by a vision revealing to him, Man and the physical world are but representations of the unseen Spiritual world. When mankind conceptualizes their spiritual identity, this physical world will reveal Infinite Potential to them, and nothing will be impossible, for when they speak, God is the speaker through them. He attended Luther Rice College and Seminary to procure a Master of Divinity degree. Is a graduate of Dale Carnegie University, and teacher of the Power of Thought, "The World Is Mental", purveyor of the idea that as images of God on earth, our involution becomes our evolution. He is the Minister and founder of Living With Abundance Ministries, broadcasting live on his YouTube channel: "Living With Abundance Ministries." Is living with Abundance as an Executive Director in healthcare, and author of the popular and intriguing book, "ADAM Man Convoluted, but GOD, which teaches the meaning of the Christ Within; Adam is the Atom in God.

www.ingramcontent.com/pod-product-compliance
Lightning Source LLC
Chambersburg PA
CBHW070543090426
42735CB00013B/3060